JOURNEY OF A
MUIZENBERG BOY

JOURNEY OF A
MUIZENBERG BOY

BARRY JOHN COHEN

FOR MY CHILDREN

Rory Joshua & Jenna Kayla

BY THE SAME AUTHOR

Blazing the Trail: This sport collector's volume chronicles the impact black golf had on overcoming discrimination, their history, and how they broke down the apartheid barriers.

Let me Play: This is the story of Papwa Sewgolum who rose from humble beginnings to challenge the might of the golfing titans on an equal footing, and after winning three Dutch Opens and two Natal Opens beating Gary Player, he was banned from playing in white tournaments and his passport withdrawn.

Let The Storm Burst: 1895. A group of trekkers travel by wagon through the bushveld to the goldfields. Romance, adventure, and a plot to overthrow the Boer Republic.

The Boys from Bulawayo: Two former Rhodesians, help a mother on the run with her twins who were being sexually abused by hiding them for four years. They are arrested and the Australian Federal Police throw the book at them. A challenging legal drama: a Family Court order or the rights of the children?

The Cedric Kushner Story: Cedric, a New York Hall of Fame Boxing recipient who arrived in the USA with $400 and broke the mould by following his passion insofar as organising and promoting musicians, bands, and boxers at the very highest level and ignoring the naysayers who look at school reports to gauge potential. We are all good at something. We just have to find our passion. Cedric was such a man.

Papwa: Against all odds, discovered at 27, taken abroad, he wins the Dutch Open 3 times, 2nd in the SA Open, and wins the Natal Open 2 times beating Gary Player and becoming the figurehead of the anti-apartheid movement only to be banned from playing and his passport withdrawn to prevent him from traveling abroad.

CONTENTS

PROLOGUE

As the war raged in Rhodesia we were able to get five-to-one on the illegal exchange rate. What an opportunity to go there on holiday, risk be damned. I was young, and it only cost R5 for a Victoria Falls room at a leading hotel as they just tried to keep hotels operational.

1976, a hot winter morning. The ground below looked like the grain of wood dark green, with patches of green. Outside nothing moved except an African cyclist. A troop of wildebeest remained stationary near the windmill as the shadow of a plane passed overhead.

I was in the cockpit when the pilot turned to me and said *"Why don't you take over the controls?"*. Well, I had never flown a 16-passenger plane before and soon realised that the air has no road or path on which to keep you steadily trundling towards your destination, so for the next hour, I had the privilege of flying a commercial aeroplane.

The plane touched down at the little airport in the bush. There was a hum in the stationary air, and the twitter of three birds playing with each other. I was back in Africa, back to the birds, to my animals, and my life. Outside the Victoria Falls airport a number of airway officials were busy with their drinks laughing as we sauntered by. One girl sat at the Hertz Car Hire looking bored as if she didn't really expect any of the passengers from the little Air Rhodesian Dakaota to hire a car. The flow of visitors to the Victoria Falls had decreased to a trickle as the ters (terrorists) had already bombarded the tiny tourist *dorp* a number of times.

It was good to be in the real Africa, not westernise Cape Town and my studies. The thought crossed my mind that I was home at last as I boarded the Kombi which was taking us to the Azambezi River Lodge situated on the Zambezi river. Inside sat an attractive woman who couldn't have been older than thirty. She was talking with a

10

German-South African accent, probably from South West Africa (Namibia). Anyway, she looked like someone I could approach, and a smile creased my face.

Some folks' lives seem to roll along smoothly. They have a clear idea of the direction, confidence, and somehow, navigate the tides, setting sail and catching the wind. Others, for whatever reason, are distracted, don't seem to think ahead, trust in the wind, and go to sleep at the wheel. The wind turns into a storm and they get shipwrecked through no real fault of their own. Every once in a while, rarely, they are washed up on a deserted island where a treasure chest awaits.

Having a smooth sail doesn't always translate into achieving exciting experiences and meeting interesting people. Maybe there is plenty of money for holidays and great times together with friends, but have you achieved your potential, anything that made a difference, influenced the lives of others?

So it was, that my friends and I grew up privileged in apartheid South Africa, seen by many in the outside world as very strange and unfair. Most 'whites' were simply unaware of what was going on. The media was totally controlled by the Afrikaner government, as were the police and army. Whites, coloured (people of mixed-race) and blacks all lived in their separate areas never to be visited by the other, unless, of course, you worked in a white area or employed maids at home.

Most white household had a maid, and I was lucky, as our maid's name was Maria Petersen, whose husband had abandoned her with her three children and her sister's child. They all lived in one room and one bathroom adjoining the house, despite the fact that it was illegal for more than one person to live on the premises.

This was brought home following a neighbour's complaint when police knocked on the door and demanded to see our maid's permit. Later my affection for Maria was such that she became my second mother and I her special child. When Willy, her son married, he introduced his new wife, Magdalene to my parents. When Maria's daughters, Rosy and Susie, got married, their husbands-to-be asked my father for permission if they could marry them. The Petersens were part of our family.

Eventually Maria and my mom became best friends. When we all went to Australia in 1983, she came with as she didn't want us to leave without her, although she did return to her children six months later when she was homesick.

Although we lived comfortably, and we only once financially able to go away on holiday to Durban when I was 13, and where I met my girlfriend, 11-year-old Janice Shapiro.

Back in Cape Town Janice and I went to the movies at the Monte Carlo on the Foreshore, but when I went to pay, I realised I didn't have enough money. Peeping around the corner was her mom and she fronted the movie tickets and refreshment. I put my arm around Janice's shoulder during the film, a daring move. A few years later I accompanied her to her school dance at Herzlia, and today living in Sydney we are still close friends.

We had the means to employ hired help and those of colour greeted us as baas (boss) or klein-baas (little boss).

Apartheid (Afrikaans for separateness) was a system of institutionalised racial segregation that existed in South Africa and South West Africa (Namibia) from 1948 to the early 1990s. Apartheid was characterised by an authoritarian political culture based on baasskap (boss-hood), which ensured that South Africa was dominated politically, socially, and economically by the nation's dominant minority white population. According to this system of social stratification, white citizens had the highest status, followed by Indians and Coloureds, then Black Africans.

Between 1960 and 1983, 3.5 million black Africans were removed from their homes and forced into segregated neighbourhoods, in some of the largest mass evictions in modern history. Most of these targeted removals were intended to restrict the black population to ten designated "tribal homelands", also known as bantustans, four of which became nominally independent states such that relocated persons lost their South African citizenship as they were absorbed into the bantustans.

During the 1970s and 1980s, internal resistance to apartheid became increasingly militant, prompting brutal crackdowns by the National Party ruling government and protracted sectarian violence that left thousands dead or in detention. Some reforms of the apartheid system were undertaken, including allowing for Indian and Coloured political representation in parliament, but these measures failed to appease the black majority.

In 1990, prominent ANC figures such as Nelson Mandela were released from prison. Apartheid legislation was repealed on 17 June 1991, leading to multiracial elections in April 1994, and Mandela as its first black President.

I was certainly aware of the inequality perpetuated by apartheid but for some reason it was not at the forefront of my consciousness, possibly because we never ventured into a black area or outside of the golf course. We seldom met or were friends with folk of colour.

I recall my father's driver, Sidwell, hid in his city Barrack Street offices while crowds marched in anger at the 1960 Sharpeville massacre, but I was only eight. The question was always *"What can we do"*.

Later golf caddies like Ivan were my friends and played golf with me when we were out of sight of the clubhouse, whilst Maria was loved just like my mom, and her children were my brother and sisters... well not really, but kind of.

I always expected life would be easy. Going from a top school, playing in the rugby, golf, and cross-country teams, and being one of the boys, then onto the army where I gained some recognition from the Afrikaner instructors due to my running and boxing, and where I was a crack shot.

From Oudtshoorn it was off to Madimbu (near Messina) on the Limpopo River border between South Africa, Mozambique, and Zimbabwe, and where we were indoctrinated that the Ruskies and Cubans were our enemies[1] and we must hate them!

Onto the University of Cape Town (UCT) where attending my first demonstration in 1972 at St. George's Cathedral. I got caught when white police charged and attacked students for the first time, including those who ran into the cathedral, and beat them over the altar.

We were demonstrating for free education for all, given that blacks had to pay for their books. Welcome to apartheid South Africa! The following days the police lined up with growling dogs at the bottom of the university Jameson stairs while 200 of us students sat on the stairs with 5000 students lined on each side, and where they proceeded to carry us off. I ran back up the stairs only for them to come after me.

President BJ Vorster had called the leader of the Student Representative Council (SRC), Jeff Budlender[2], all kinds of derogatory names, to which Budlender inside a packed Jameson Hall rejected his insinuations, *"with the contempt they deserve".*

---

1   Now South Africa loves them and the former allies now appear to be the enemy. Go figure…

2   Geoffrey Budlender SC is known for his involvement in public interest litigation. He co-founded the Legal Resources Centre, where he worked as an attorney until he was admitted as an advocate in 2005. He is currently a part-time member of the Competition Commission's

Student life had some fun elements like playing rugby for Law and going on rugby tours. One such tour with the university Chancellor, Sir Richard Luyt's, daughter, Fran Luyt in the party, landed up at Fort Hare University (for blacks) where we were informed that all white students had been banned from the university campus, but as we had not been informed about the banning, we were welcome.

We then had a political debate concerning the future of the country, legal students on both sides (in our party Ray McLarty was to become a judge, Hugh Corder the faculty Emeritus Law Professor, and Fran Luyt a respected Law Academic. No doubt others excelled) where Steve Biko[3] basically informed us that they wanted a clear polarisation between white and black, and that they didn't want the support of white liberal students as they muddied the water (I don't think we really understood who Biko was). I suppose the brake came off after that and I no longer involved myself with politics.

Immediately after graduating with good final year grades. I received top offers from worldwide branded businesses and law firms such that I was sure my career and expectations would be met, no doubt I would be financially well off, especially after the way I was treated by members at my golf club. I had a glittering future ahead of me. Girls liked me. However, life had other plans...

Deep down I carried a great deal of insecurity concerning my intelligence and ability. I would tease that the person who came

---

3   Stephen Biko was an anti-apartheid activist. Ideologically an African nationalist and African socialist, he was at the forefront of a grassroots anti-apartheid campaign known as the Black Consciousness Movement during the late 1960s and 1970s. He became a leading figure in the creation of the South African Students' Organisation (SASO) in 1968. Membership was open only to all "blacks". He was careful to keep his movement independent of white liberals, but opposed anti-white hatred and had white friends. His assassination 04/09/1977 nearly sparked a civil war.

below me at school would fail, just to make me feel that little bit better. Then I hit the wall studying law, failing subjects every year as I turned my attention to fine art.

Still, I had now hoisted my sail and was keen to see where the wind would take me, hopefully not far from my roots. I was now on my magical mystery tour which in my wildest dreams I could not have foreseen, yes, maybe for my clever friends but not for me.

Then life intervened. Instead of going left I went right, instead of taking the high road I took the low road, and I had to learn how to cope with all sorts of highs and lows, such as depression and unrequited love, but every time I sunk beneath the waves I somehow bobbed cork-like, back up to the surface. Mostly it was not my fault but life doesn't care about that. If you are in the path of a cyclone, you get blown away.

All the time, subconsciously gravitating towards my passion and areas of work which appealed to me even if this was not my training. My folks sent me three times to be assessed by a career guidance psychologist and each time I came away with a report that *"he is creative"*, to which my folks responded *"rubbish, he has shown no such aptitude"*, but then we never had creative subjects at school. So, it was law for me.

But even then, before I proceeded with law articles, I went to work for Readers Digest: book division as an assistant product manager.

At the same time, it's important to ignore the naysayers who tell you it can't be done if you believe in the project. Maybe I was just too naïve not to recognise the downside and the difficulties. Of course, I would succeed, and yes, I could do it. Yeah right! There's some 'fortune', or 'luck' as people are wanting to call it.

CHAPTER 1
MUIZENBERG: The early days

"What counts in life is not the mere fact that we have lived. It is what difference we have made to the lives of others that will determine the significance of the life we lead" – NELSON MANDELA

Muizenberg started as a place for holiday homes for the rich after the discovery of gold on the Witwatersrand in 1886. A beach-side town in the Western Cape, situated where the shore of the Cape Peninsula curves round to the east on the False Bay coast, and currently home to the Cape Town surfing community, centred on the popular 'Surfer's Corner'.

I was born at 5:30 pm with the slopes of Table Mountain ablaze on the best day of the year, the 14th of February, Valentine's Day!

The day became associated with romantic love in the 14th and 15th centuries when notions of courtly love flourished, apparently by association with the "lovebirds" of early spring. In 18th-century England, it grew into an occasion for couples to express their love for each other by presenting flowers, confectionery, and sending valentine cards which include heart-shaped symbols, doves, and the figure of the winged Cupid.

Would I expect a life of romance and happy angels playing harps, and was I my mother's valentines present?

What was special was that I always received postcards on the 14th and wondered whether the postman would be thinking that I had a lot of Valentine romantic interest.

Long before the turn of the 20th century, many of the gold and diamond barons of the country had holiday homes in Muizenberg, below the mountain. There was JB Robinson[4] and his daughter Countess Labia, Abe Bailey, John Garlick, Schlesinger (on the beach front), Sammy Marks, Alpheus Williams, and even the mighty Cecil John Rhodes himself had cottages, or mansions, in Muizenberg.

With hazy, lazy days of summer, talent contests at the pavilion, endless rolling calm waves from the warm Indian Ocean, and the famous "snake pit" where bathers would squeeze in to protect themselves from the southeaster wind sandstorms. Jewish kids flocked to the 'Snake Pit' in the hope of meeting their future summer romance partner and where lifelong friendships were made.

Muizenberg, 'Snake Pit' 1964 where we all hung out

---

4   **Louis Cohen**, one-time Barney Barnato partner, wrote a very funny scandalous book *'Reminiscences of Kimberley'* for which JB Robinson obtained a court injunction stopping publication on the grounds of libel such that only 15 copies were printed. Countess Labia, his daughter, subsequently unsuccessfully sued my father for his copy, which I now own.

The soft white sand that seemed to go on for miles; the sea that found that perfect sweet spot of being calm enough for swimming but full of waves enough for some surfing at the corner with upcoming legends like Gavin Rudolph and sometimes Shaun Tomson; and the rows of those famous bright multi-colour changing boxes gave the whole beach a weirdly homely feel.

The Johannesburg guys and girls arrived in December after school broke up, then the Rhodesians, followed by the locals. With over 650 Muizenberg Jewish families, we were the best of the rest.

All of this was hidden just behind the town's famous pavilion and its amusement park attractions, playing putt-putt before checking out the trampolines, exercise on the lawns, and the boats, with the clan playing bok-bok, teenage beauty contests which Lenella Lemkus, with her long golden hair won, future boxing and music legend, Cedric Kushner[5] playing beach bats with Jeff Schneider and his booming laughter, touch rugby irrespective of your age, and Vic Davis playing his clarinet in the morning for the younger kids and a sweetie for going onto the stage, late afternoons bopping on the windmill dance floor.

Maybe fishing in the *Zandvlei* with dough for bait or placing it in a bottle into which the fish swam, playing marbles down Windermere Road, making canoes out of corrugate iron, racing your bike with a playing card attached to the wheel spokes, or collecting Coca-Cola

---

5 **Cedric Kushner**, NY Boxing Hall of Fame 2016 was one of the most significant promoters in the sport in the '80s and early 2000s. Boxers he promoted and/or managed included Hasim Rahman when he beat Lennox Lewis for the undisputed world title, Sugar Shnae Msley, pound for pound the best fighter when he beat Oscar de la Hoy, Shannon Briggs, Oleg Maskaev, Chris Byrd, Corrie Sanders, Ike Ibeabuchi and David Tua. He was also a major music promoter including most major bands and artists like Fleetwood Mac, Doobie Brothers, the Rolling Stones, and AC/DC which he also managed for a time.

bottles, for which the local shop, *Crowders*, down the road on Princess George's Drive would pay a penny for. With our earnings we bought sweeties, and argue whether Cliff Richard or Elvis Presley was better.

On Saturdays it was amateur boxing in the beachside pavilion, or motorbike scrambling on the dunes, or it was off to the morning Empire bioscope *skop, skiet en donner* western, where we swapped comics at interval (Little Lotto for Archie or Richie Rich) and bought a six-pence (5c) *stuk* (piece) of biltong next door. If you didn't have a shilling (10 cents) you snuck into the toilets, emerging at interval to see the main cowboy feature to the welcoming screams of young voices; otherwise, it was a 35-minute walk to Kalk Bay and the Olympia bio and a double-feature where for only eight-pence you sat downstairs while the mixed-race kids seated upstairs threw water bombs down at you.

Later surfing at the corner with my 9' 6" Whitmore surfboard; On Sunday nights we took in variety concerts at the pavilion with Vic Davis hosting the concert.

For some reason I used to see photos of myself in the newspaper starting from when I was 6 in sub-A (grade R) ogling at some fashion models. I had taste! Then winning my first cup for canoeing at 10 with my friend Stephen Geffen, and then again, every now and then mostly for golf.

Saturday was watching rugby at Newlands and my team, False Bay. Especially when there was a rugby test match, like the All Blacks in 1960 led by Wilson Whineray with Don Clark kicking (he married a local Jo'burg girl and relocated) and the 1962 Lions Tour with captain Arthur Smith and Richard Sharp.

We would take our sleeping bag and cloths to school and then dawdle down to the Newlands rugby stadium lining up along the fence and unrolling our bedding, put on our warm track suites, buy

Stephen Geffen, D. Saunders (Pres. Cape of Good Hope Rotary Club), Barry Cohen for winning double canoe race. Barry also won the singles canoe race.

hot dogs from the vendor, and chat with friends late into the night. The was no such thing as parents checking up or being concerned about safety, and the next morning the gates would open at 09:00 and we would charge into the scholar enclosure where the preliminary school games would commence followed by more significant curtain-raisers. Came the test match and many of us would be asleep. Then there was still the train ride back to False Bay station and a walk home.

During the week some touring players and even Springboks would visit our school and chat to us kids, and we would dream of becoming a Springbok.

Meantime, my sister Lindsay was selling programmes at the stadium for school welfare fundraising and managed to get a number of Springboks to sign autographs for me. She was in my good book the whole week. That was before she became a *'flower power'* child.

However, it was not always fun as one day when I was fifteen, I was crossing the *vlei* foot bridge when I noticed people standing on the bank and a coloured youth lying in the water. I jumped in, hauling him to the bank and tried artificial resuscitation, but I never gave him mouth-to-mouth as there was foam coming out. He had passed on.

Meanwhile the Beatles were banned after John Lennon stated they were more popular than Jesus, as were songs like Santana's *'Black Magic Woman'*, Jeremy Taylor's *'Ag please daddy'*, and of course J.J. Cale's *'Cocaine'*. We listened to these on LM radio. Later it was Rodrigues with *'Cold Fact'*, the theme rebellion record of my student days.

At 12, I discovered golf quite by chance after I went one Sunday afternoon, I went to watch my dad go lawn bowling at Clovelly CC where it so happened, they were hosting the Western Province professional golf championship and it wasn't long before I was playing.

I instantly thought I was a great putter, and when Putt-Putt opened next to the beach in December 1964, I was their first paying customer and became the Muizenberg putting champion winning various tournaments.

The first major event was open to all with qualifying on the course closest to the beach. I managed to make the morning cut and went home for Saturday lunch all excited as I changed into my blue 'uniform', and returned to do battle on the other course.

After I took the lead at the end of round one, around 600 people were following me including my dad and sister. I managed to hold my nerve through round two and won the tournament, winning a reel-to-reel tape recorder. Well, that was the last time I saw the recorder until my sister Lindsay returned it broken. But at least I saw my name in the newspaper and American Putt-Putt magazines.

Fortune came when I was given a Shetland sheep dog (smaller colouring and version of Lassie) by neighbours returning to New Zealand, who would follow me wherever I went. Man's best friend, and his name was Rory, just like my son.

Come Guy Fawkes, the community would all wait in the parking lot area along Zandvlei at the beach while the adults let off spectacular firework displays. We were entranced and enthralled by the Catherine Wheels and rockets bursting stars into the night sky, as long as the South-Easter wind didn't blow.

On a weekly basis in summer there would be a social at the Herzl Hall where 1000 mainly Jewish kids converged for a twist session to the Alpha Set, Omega Limited, Jimmy Retief of the Idiots playing his guitar with his teeth, Shag, The Square Set, Nu Trend, and McCully Workshop. Sunday nights also included concerts at the Beach Pavilion, where Max Collie hypnotised anyone going onto the stage, including future Muizenberg legend Boxing Hall of Famer, Cedric Kushner, having him run around the concert hall barking like a dog trying to catch his 'tail' (Cedric would later have the task of barking like a dog before Fleetwood Mac would allow him promote some of their concerts).

23

At 23, Cedric landed in America with $400 in his pocket and was to go on to promote and manage a host of famous bands, including The Rolling Stones, Queen, AC/DC, The Doobie Brothers, Fleetwood Mac, and many more, and thereafter promote over 300 world boxing title fights including world boxing champions Hasim Rahman who knocked out Lennox Lewis for the world heavyweight title and Sugar Shane Mosley when he defeated Oscar de la Hoya.

Meanwhile, another local legend, Colin Goodman started the night club, *The Back Door*, upstairs across the road from the Empire, which sadly didn't last long due to the lack of permits, whilst intellectually challenged 'R16' (Ralph Levy) held court at the Empire bio.

Ralph's parents were millionaires in the 1920s living in Royal Road, one road back from the beachfront. When Ralph was six years old when he was struck with meningitis, and despite traveling the world to find a cure, Ralph was left retarded with a clinical six-year-old age. Meanwhile he grew broad, strong, and over six foot.

Twice a week (Wednesday and Saturday) he would go to the bioscope, always wearing a suit and tie, where they kept a seat for him, R16, and where the kids would mercilessly tease him to await his loud reaction, which came in the form of *"shut up, shut up, shut up"* as he rose up from his seat.

Over the years, this sweet, kind man-boy became possibly Muizenberg's best-known citizen, and is regularly recalled today on Facebook posts, followed by apologies for his taunting.

We were lucky, we had everything youngsters could want: sport, romance, girls and fast cars. On Friday nights our crowd bundled into Scotty Gerson's open van and it was off to watch Hellenic at Hartleyvale (sometimes Cape Town City). Hellenic were glamorous because they had a string of overseas professionals in

German international Steffenhagen (right) playing for Hellenic FC against Cape Town City at Hartleyvale, in the early 1970s

their ranks, including England players George Eastham, Gordon Banks, and Budgie Byrnes, and banned German footballers, German international Arno Stefenhagen, Erich Geyer, Wolfgang Weber, and Volker Gross. The Germans had been temporarily banned for taking bribes at Ajex Amsterdam and had ventured south to play domestically in South Africa while their banning order elapsed.

I was schooled at South Africa's oldest school, the liberal boys-only South African College School (SACS) founded in 1828, the old-fashioned school was both full of tradition and almost a sporting academy, and which high school my uncle Lionel (architect) rebuilt in 1960 at Newlands (previously situated in Orange Street, Cape Town), where I followed in the footsteps of my grandfather (Salisbury Chief Justice) and my uncle.

I was clearly brought up on a diet of sport, especially as there were no art-related or creative subjects at school, not that I thought I was inclined in that direction at that time, even though I enjoyed the creative side.

The only teacher who took an interest in me was John Ince (my history teacher and rugby coach), who told my parents I was a late developer, and who I recall being as surprised as my friend, Trevor Zabow, as I emerged out of the forest and into the school cross-country team ahead of most of the 200 participating boys, whilst Mr. Smith, our English teacher heaped praise on an essay I had written concerning my three-year older sister turning from an ugly duckling into a swan as suddenly I noticed she was popular with the boys.

Smith saw some potential in me. He left a note for me to have a chat with him. Needless to say, I never had that chat. But what did he see that no one else saw?

But school inculcated a competitive spirit, and I enjoyed participating and winning. By high school, I was already excelling at golf, while playing fairly decent rugby, swimming, then running competitive cross-country, training every day with my friends Howard Oblowitz, Rodney and Jeffery Melmed, trying to outpace them, cutting across the traffic as we came across the Muizies car bridge, but never quite succeeding, and then there was always surfing.

Meanwhile, I would try to hide away at the back of the class dreaming of the moment the bell would ring and we could get on with sport.

School left me with some amazing friends which have lasted a lifetime, such that today we still have a cyberclub of some of these old friends around the world and chat weekly. For the rest, it left me with an academic inferiority complex. If you suffered from attention deficit disorder (ADD), as I suspect I did, it certainly went undiagnosed.

1969 School dance: Mervyn Shein, Barry Cohen, Avra Jacobson, Jonathan Pinshaw, Avril Beinart

After matriculating from SACS, still seventeen, it was off to the army for compulsory military service. But still, I mustn't grumble, I was billeted at boiling hot Oudtshoorn, where we ran up sand dunes with heavy poles bouncing on our shoulders. After that we were posted to Madimbu (near Messina) on the South African, Mozambique, and Rhodesian border where terrorist incursions were only just commencing.

Fortunately, some of my school and Muizenberg friends were also sent there so it wasn't so bad when your bed wasn't tossed out the window or the Jewish boys had to do an extra hour of drill. Everything was in Afrikaans and our instructors were Afrikaners, the first time I had come in contact with them. None of us wanted to be there as we didn't support the Nationalist Party and its Apartheid regime.

In a way I was fortunate because being quite fit I came second in their cross-country trials beating all but one Afrikaans boy, and I boxed. That was until I hurt someone and apologised, for which I was *kaked* out (told off).

I also got away for weekends pretending to play in fictitious golf tournaments, reporting that I only came third, knowing they wouldn't check-up. I was even in favour as sharpshooter with an LMG machine gun (like Stallone in 'First Blood') until I 'killed' our entire platoon at the infantry trials when I never heard the command to stop firing.

However, eventually the leader of our crack unit, Eris Haysamen left a message one day on my bed. It read: *"Barry, jy is die mooiste Jood wat ek al ooit ontmoet het, maar jy is tog soe lui."* (Barry you are the nicest Jew I have ever met, but you are so very lazy).

After completing my compulsory military service, it was back to the land of the living, with no-one screaming commands at you, While still a teenager, in late December 1971 I organised a music concert with the help of a few others titled *'Folk Plus'*, on an island in Zandvlei connected by a bridge adjoining the Tops' boathouse

1970 infantry. Barry Cohen protecting South Africa on the SA, Rhodesian, Mozambique border at Madimbu

and restaurant, in aid of Leos (Young Lions).

Using a squeegee, we made up black and white posters which we attached to the highway poles (without obtaining municipal approval), contacted some bands and musicians whilst pleading poverty and charity.

We were surprised how readily they were prepared to perform and show off their musical talents as long as we covered their basic expenses.

After the first few groups agreed to play, the word got around and suddenly there was a deluge of prominent groups wanting to perform including Amanda (Cohen) Blue Leigh[6] & HAMMAK (with Andre de Villiers, and Anton Fig[7] on drums), Peter Wale's Wakeford Heart, David Nissen, Amanda Berman, and Woodstock performing band South Country Band, with Tully McCully (from the popular recording group McCully Workshop) doing the sound, and Paul Zammek the compere, all for the grand total of R250 (about $170 in those days).

We were hoping for 500 paying concert goers to attend, but were concerned that the southeaster wind would be pumping with

---

6   **Amanda Cohen**. Whilst still a school girl at San Souci girls high school in Newlands, Cape Town, Amanda's wealthy Bishopscourt father was sentenced to 12 years in jail for killing her mother. Amanda has been the lead singer of several bands, writing her own material, her rock/soul/blues roots, most notably her band SPIDER with drummer Anton Fig. In the 80's, SPIDER went on to tour with Alice Cooper, and Tina Turner covered the SPIDER original, "Better Be Good to Me" which took home Best Female Rock Vocal Performance at the 27th Grammy Awards (1985). In the 90's, Amanda played with Noel Redding (Hendrix) and was managed by Gene Simmons (KISS). You can listen to 'HAMMAK Live' on youtube

7   **Anton Fig**. Best known as the drummer for Paul Shaffer and the World's Most Dangerous Band. David Letterman, for whom the band served as house band on his late-night talk shows. Fig is also well known for his work with Kiss, Ace Frehley and Joe Bonamassa.

Amanda Cohen performing with HAMMAK

its usual summer ferocity. Although it was a windy day and (an exceptionally) windy night 5,000 people pitched up, paying their R10 entry fee, and there was beautiful Merle Lifson with her extremely long golden hair below her knees, who was to follow me most of my life, being pursued by a posse of young men.

Soon thereafter, now with long hair, I was attending Cape Town University, and my first demonstration for free education for black students at St Georges Cathedral in 1972 when the police charged us with truncheons and dogs. It was the first time the police had gone for white students. The following day I was carried off the university Jameson stairs by these same apartheid police. Oh, what fun!

The police lined up with dogs at the bottom of the stairs, and a 'crazy or brave' school friend, David Charlaff sat right under these dogs snapping at him, while I was further up. Carried off, I ran back up the stairs again, but this time they came for me and were not so gentle.

My parents weren't impressed. They were worried I would get into trouble with the security police, especially after photos of me handing out pamphlets started circulating around campus with a red ring around my face. With my long hair and, droopy moustache, I was the typical '*betooger*' (demonstrator) against the apartheid state.

Girlfriends, well, yes, I used to ask out all the attractive ones, and they came, but then I was so very shy. I hardly said a word and I wouldn't ask them out again in case they refused. How stupid was that?

What really happened in the cathedral on Friday?

Barry Cohen (1971)

JUNE 2, 1972, was a day Cape Town should remember: a peaceful UCT student protest outside St George's Cathedral to bring home to the public some of the injustices of apartheid education, including such things as the discrimination in the amount paid for White and Black students was attacked by the SA Police (SAP): the first occasion in South Africa where white students had been physically attacked and injured in significant numbers during any political demonstration.

Students demonstrating on the steps of St. George's Cathedral, Cape Town in the misguided belief that, because it was private property and a church, they would be safe, were baton-charged. Fifty-one students were charged with breaking municipal regulations. Further protests in Cape Town city were banned under the Riotous Assemblies Act, 1956 and a protest about the police action, again on St George's Cathedral steps, was dispersed with tear gas and rubber batons.

A further protest, this time on the steps of Jameson Hall at the University of Cape Town ("UCT") was also dispersed by the police with rubber batons, dogs and tear-gas. The Council of UCT under the leadership of the principal and vice-chancellor, Sir Richard Luyt, obtained an interdict to prevent the police entering its private property.

In the course of these protests a large number of students were arrested and charged under the Riotous Assemblies Act. Some were convicted by magistrates but later acquitted on appeal.

Some students, funded by the National Union of South African Students ("NUSAS") took the government to court and obtained out of court settlements, which were given to NUSAS.

Because most of the students involved were shocked and frightened at the time, and some were bleeding as a result of having been assaulted, it is almost impossible to reconstruct a second-by-second account of what happened in St George's Cathedral on Friday afternoon.

UCT students numbering perhaps 200 were sitting on Cathedral main steps protesting about racial inequalities in education. After a discussion between police colonel Pieter Crous and Dirk Kemp, a student leader (former 1969 SACS head boy) over the use of a loud-hailer, a large squad of policemen suddenly baton-charged the students. The attack instruction was given by Brigadier Martinus Lamprecht, who later appeared in a series of Cape Times photographs watching a snarling police sergeant club a student already sprawled on the pavement. Interviewed on the spot, in a shaken, trembling voice Lamprecht stated that the protest had become a "public meeting" and "these people refused to move, so I gave the order to disperse them".

The police beatings were witnessed by thousands of members of the public and over the following days received widespread press coverage.

What particularly shocked bystanders and journalists was the sheer hate demonstrated by the police towards the students. Mostly in their late teens and early 20s, the students were mercilessly beaten regardless of gender, several suffering injuries requiring hospitalisation. The police pursued students into the cathedral, grabbing women by their hair and hurling them down the outside stairs into the street when the police charged with batons about 4 pm. About 100 students immediately fled through the north transept into the cathedral.

The Latin inscription on these doors reads: *'I am the door: by Me if any man enters in, he shall be saved.'*

The doors were closed behind them. Within all was illuminated only by the late afternoon sun filtering through the cathedral's vast stained-glass windows high overhead. There were echoes of shouts, and the screams of those still being attacked outside.

Inside the students felt safe. A cathedral was inviolate. The police would not continue their beatings and baton assaults here. They thought themselves also safe from those they called 'Muller's muggers' – policemen dressed in garb apparently designed to make them look like students.

There was a scuffle at a side door, from which steps lead down to a parking bay marked: 'Reserved for the Archbishop.' Police charged up these steps and burst into the cathedral, dashing past the granite font and spreading into the transept crossing. The assaults inside the cathedral began.

Students fled. A few followed Catherine King, 20-year-old daughter of the Dean of Cape Town, whose intimate knowledge of the building led her to the concealed seclusion of the organ loft high above the choir, where they remained.

Others ran into the nave, pursued by shouting policemen. Rows of chairs collapsed, the police swore, but the students continued to run, dodging behind pillars.

Some fled up the chancel steps, through the choir towards the High Altar and the Sanctuary, in the belief that they would be safe here, beyond the giant Archbishops throne, which was once part of the organ screen in England's historic 'Westminster Abbey.

At least two policemen followed them up here. One of the students was punched and beaten as he scrambled over the choir stalls, and he was followed up to the Sanctuary as he made for the High Altar.

He was dragged by the hair as he called out *'I haven't done anything.'* He was dragged over the small stone which bears nothing but the name office and dates of birth and death of Archbishop Geoffrey Clayton, whose ashes were interred here in accordance with his wishes to be buried in a place where there was no colour bar.

This student was pushed out to the side door to the police on the steps outside, where he was again beaten. Other policemen near the font were dragging students out to the door, and batons were used on them.

One assault took place in the nave of the cathedral.

It was at this point that Canon R. M. Jeffrey, senior chaplain to the archbishop heard screams coming from within the cathedral and came through the north transept. Police were dragging students past him out the door to those who waited outside to assault them.

Canon Jeffery made himself known to the man who appeared to him to be the senior uniformed man present and ordered the police out of his church. A minute later the police had left the cathedral, but students who tried to get out any of the doors were still attacked.

Students were initially led out by concealed entrances in groups of twos and threes until about 40 were left. Helen Suzman. Progressive Party MP for Houghton led some out. Japie Basson, United Party MP for Bezuidenhout (later to become Bezuidenhout Valley), had police removed from the western entrance, where students wished to leave.

Among scores of people arrested during the day were at least three clergymen, including the Dean of St. George's, the Rev. Edward L. King. Dean King and two other Cape Town clerics, the Rev. Theo Kotze, General Secretary of the South African Council of Churches, and the Rev. Bernard Wrankmore[8], a seamen's mission priest, were arrested outside the cathedral.

A shocked Anglican archbishop of Cape Town, Robert Selby Taylor, demanded a full report from the police concerning their conduct within the cathedral. Another Anglican bishop, Reverend Hollowes of Natal, compared the police and particularly the purportedly "plain clothes members" who had been prominent

---

8   **Reverend Bernie Wrankmore** went on a protest fast on Signal Hill for 67 days in 1971. The Anglican priest captured the imagination of thousands of Capetonians. He aimed to fast until the apartheid government opened an inquest into the death in detention of Muslim cleric and Imam of the al Jamia Mosque in Claremont, Abdullah Haron. It never did. His health seriously compromised, Wrankmore finally gave up his fast. At 73 he took up surfing at Muizenberg to the delight of the youngsters.

among the assaulters, as akin to the violent role played historically by Adolf Hitler's Brownshirts. Students had been clubbed in the Sanctuary under the High Altar by policemen swearing and clearly out of control.

The following day, a further protest, this time on the steps of Jameson Hall at UCT was also dispersed by the police with rubber batons, dogs and tear-gas. The Council of UCT under the leadership of the principal and vice-chancellor, Sir Richard Luyt, obtained an interdict to prevent the police entering its private property.

In the ensuing weeks, small groups of students (to avoid constituting an illegal assembly) stood on a building in the Rose Garden of UCT, overlooking De Waal Drive, to continue the protest.

In the course of these protests a large number of students were arrested and charged under the Riotous Assemblies Act. Some were convicted by magistrates but later acquitted on appeal. Some students, funded by the National Union of South African Students (NUSAS) took the government to court and obtained out of court settlements, which were given to NUSAS.

Then the president of NUSAS, Neville Curtis, had to flee over the mountains into Lesotho, and onto New Zealand and then Tasmania to avoid being arrested.

In reality, the students and police, indeed the police and most of Cape Town's southern suburbs public were culturally poles apart. Despite the beating incidents occurring when apartheid was at its most intense, the students shared citizenship and even a common "apartheid white race classification" with the police, but that was where commonalities ended. The students represented liberal and "radical" white English South African middle-class youth, drawn mostly from comfortable backgrounds and imbibed with the idealism of sixties, early seventies' Western students. They believed social and political conditions could be changed through protest and activism. The police demonstrated to white Southern Suburb Capetonians, most of whom were not National Party voters, just how vicious law-enforcement state agencies could be if the government was publicly confronted over its racial policies.

A protest meeting was held inside the Cathedral on June 6, addressed by a range of leading citizens, political and religious representatives, including Helen Suzman, Dean Edward King and heart surgeon Marius Barnard, whose brother Professor Chris Barnard publicly warned provincial government authorities not to threaten his brother with dismissal, or the world-famous heart transplant surgeon would himself resign from Groote Schuur Hospital.

The police attack at the cathedral succeeded in mobilising moderate UCT students who were not necessarily politically aligned or supportive of NUSAS. NUSAS at this time was strongly influenced by people like Rick Turner (later assassinated) with their Marxist-derived interpretations of apartheid being only comprehensible through class-based rather than race-based explanations.

But most of the students and public outrage was against the brutality of the police, the ugly side of which was generally completely hidden from the white middle-class residents of Cape Town. The SAP members involved were also mostly young and grew up in markedly different social environments from average UCT students.

Virtually all Afrikaners, the policemen were the products of a community which, by 1972, were almost exclusively government supporters and had benefited from the aggressive Afrikanisation of the civil service since 1948. Even long before this date, the police service had been an attraction for working-class Afrikaner men and a catchment point for Nationalist supporters and even more extreme right-wingers. Raised through the cultural autarky of Afrikaans schools, government-supporting churches, the SA Police College and unquestioning obedience to authority, police officers reflected the National Party's acute suspicion of "English" youth influenced by what they clumsily understood as permissive, "hippie", "communistic" student culture emanating from Britain and the United States. If some of the NUSAS-supporting students represented the most extreme left of white South African political thinking in 1972, their police assailants definitely represented local versions of jackbooted right-wing Nazi storm troopers, whose minds were drenched in Afrikaner-nationalist propaganda. Emboldened with full state authority, the police laid into *"Kommunistiese Engelse hippies"*.

The fact that a central Anglican building of worship had also been so defiled cut no ice with Prime Minister John Vorster who was quoted as saying he was *"proud of my police"* and he warned English-language universities *"to get their house in order"* or face extreme legislative sanctions.

In Parliament, Prime Minister Vorster gave a strong warning that student demonstrators could expect more tough treatment from the Government. and told Parliament he would not hesitate to track down the militants *"and take action against them."*

He rejected a call for an official inquiry into police action against students and said he would not allow people to gain the impression that law and order could not be maintained in South Africa.

Students bludgeoned at the Cathedral
Cape Town June 2 1972 Dr Rodney Warwick

A pregnant woman was amongst those beaten in the Cathedral into which the police also attempted to throw tear gas. Outside, the

Jeopardizing privilege

The conditions that mobilized white students in June 1972 to challenge the apartheid education system in South Africa

People protest with placards on the steps of St George's Cathedral, Cape Town

Students protesting outside Jameson Hall

50-year-old wife of a National Party MP, one Yvonne Van Oudehove, who had reprimanded a policeman for assaulting a student, was smashed to the ground and arrested by a constable old enough to be her son. Bruised and dazed, according to a contemporary report, the policeman presented justified his charging of her by stating: *"Dis die tannie wat ek geslaan het"* (This is the aunty that I hit).

Our lectures for now filled with short hair special services security police, especially those of Francis Wilson (economics) and Frederick van Zyl Slabbert's (future leader of the opposition Progressive Federal Party) lectures.

Meanwhile there was much political discussion in the law moot room including Denis Davis (later Judge) and Anton Lubowski advocating for a free South West Africa, who was later assassinated.

We got television in 1976 and were glued to the screen to watch Dallas, Rich Man Poor Man, Bonanza, and in Afrikaans *'Die tier brigade'*. I was still active running three to five kilometres in the afternoons with my three friends, racing each other on the way back, then listening to the Goon show on the radio on Sundays. I also managed to find the time in all of this to learn to play the guitar.

During the December holidays, I had a Christmas-time student job at Sid Bernstein's bottle store in District Six, a world far removed from my normal reality, whilst during the year for pocket money I would drive my retarded uncle, Ralph Levy, to Camel Rock, Scarborough, twice a week for tea and scones and if I was lucky, I might also be able to get a surf.

How right the assessment by the career psychologist concerning my creativity turned out to be. I had no real interest in law besides passing, and I now discovered a talent for oil painting. Soon I had been offered a scholarship at Ruth Prowse Art Academy, studying law in the library, then onto art classes at night with lectures and painting under Eric Loubser[9], and exhibiting my paintings.

I had gone pony trekking through Lesotho, up Mount Machache and then onto the Maletsunyane Falls and excitedly picking up what

---

9   **Erik Laubscher** was not only a brilliant artist but also in the heart of art action, a spokesman, teacher and personality. His paintings became the poetic language of his emotions

turned out to be 'fools' diamonds. While riding I sketched a beautiful drawing at dawn after some rain which I later painted in a Cubism style and exhibited.

Another painting was of midnight at the docks. It depicted an eerie ship, painted with the squeal of tires and swearing as a prostitute was ejected from the car.

Meanwhile, I was failing subjects along the way, the first time I had failed at anything while my friends cruised along. My confidence disintegrated, I now felt inferior. I would be judged. I felt sure.

But then something interesting occurred. My friend Jonathan Pinshaw invited me to take part in an Old Mutual team building exercise in Franschhoek where they used students to practise on. We were placed in teams and had to complete certain tasks while competing against the other teams. Those who completed tasks with higher risks were better rewarded than those completing tasks with lower risks.

Afterwards their team interviewed each of us, and when it was my turn, they asked me how I thought I had fared out of five. I replied two. *"Oh, no, they responded you were much better than that"*. A little affirmation went a long way.

The real question now was which path was I going to take, and family persuaded me to put aside my art materials and concentrate on final year law.

Unbeknown to me, life would change my path and take me along a different route.

CHAPTER 2
GOLF a life changing challenge

Now 12-years old, January 11, 1964, one Sunday afternoon, I travelled one Sunday afternoon with my dad to Clovelly Country Club, where he was to play lawn bowls.

As we approached the club up a valley beyond Kalk Bay, lots of cars were parked on both sides of the road. I had never seen this kind of thing before. Normally I went along for the ride, gorging myself on the left-over tea-time sandwiches. Sometimes I swam in the club pool. What was going on?

Cheering rose from the golf course below the clubhouse as I made my way onto the bank above the 18th green with the Western Province Open Championship in progress.

It wasn't long before there was muttering that Gary Player had taken a seven on the par-5 ninth after Dr Cecil Goldberg gave a ruling that his tee-shot, which landed on the dirt road was out-of-bounds (according to local rules). Gary vehemently objected, stating he would never again play at Clovelly if the ruling was upheld, which it was.

Coming up the hill on the 18th was Bobby Locke[10] as his tee-shot

---

10 **'Bobby' Locke** is one of the greatest golfers of all time. He won The Open Championship four times and 15 PGA Tour events in total after which he was banned. He won over 50 significant victories in his home country, including the South African Open nine times (every time he played). was a phenomenal putter. In one year, he played 100 rounds of golf and never three-putted once!

split the fairway, drawing from right to left, his trademark shot. A crowd favourite at Clovelly where annually he regularly spent the three summer months of the year.

A graceful pivot with his right knee leading forward and a full turn of his ample body, his wedge dropped over his right shoulder on his backswing, then a powerful crisp downward turn and the ball and grass separated from the turf as it spun skywards, up the hill, pitching past the pin, then spinning back to three-foot from the pin to the rapturous applause and shouts of *"Bobby, Bobby, Bobby."* To further shouts of his nickname, *'Muffin face'*, the four-time British Open winner, strode up onto the green, tipped his white peak cap and knelt into his familiar pre-putting routine reading the green and twirling his trusty wooden blade putter. Afterwards he practised putting imitation putts again from right to left with his feet turned inwards, aiming to the right of the hole, he proceeded to clip the putt with the inside of the end of the blade hooking the putt, which he did with every shot including his putts, although I dare say I have subsequently witnessed him fade the ball when it was required.

He learnt to hook the ball from right to left to get additional run especially after fellow pros in the USA said he had a weak left hand, to which he retorted, *"Maybe so, but I take my cheques with my right hand".*

Unbeatable in the USA from 1949 – 1951 which led to him being banned for a time after some professionals complained that he was taking all the money, Locke was the undisputed Clovelly favourite. His ball settle into the hole to a roar of adulation from the crowd. This was their man, the golfer who coined the immortal phrase: *"You putt for show, but I putt for dough."*

A perroquet up onto his toes as he touched his cap again to the applause and retrieved the ball out of the hole. A final birdie.

In fact, after Sam Snead won only two out of 18 challenge matches in South Africa, he remarked that Locke could sink putts from anywhere even over peanut-butter, and the crowd went wild as he threw his ball to the gallery.

"The real success in golf lies in turning three shots into two."

Bobby Locke

Starry-eyed, I thought this was fun, exciting, and the dye was cast as Locke came 4th, Harold Henning 3rd after driving the par 4 14th and sinking his putt for an eagle two, Gary Player 2nd, and 24-year-old Retief Waltman[11], Player's heir apparent winning the title.

It was after the Masters that Waltman at 25 had beaten Locke in the first round of the 1957 South African Professional Match Play Championship. His victory was referred to as one of the greatest surprises in South African golf for several years. He was an unknown teenager and Locke was considered one of the best golfers in the world and would go on to win the British Open four months later

After returning from playing in the 1964 Masters that Waltman at 25 called time on his career, gave away his clubs and took up the calling of the church, having already been twice invited to play in the Masters, including a game with his hero, Ben Hogan.

---

11 **Retief Waltman** is a Christian missionary who won his first big tournament, the 1961 South African Open, by an extraordinary eight shots. Two years later he would win the event again by shot over Indian golfer Papwa Sewgolum. In addition to these triumphs, he won multiple other events on the South African circuit and the 1963 Dutch Open.

Nevertheless, the day seemed to belong to the maestro, *'Maaaster'* Locke, playing only five years since a train hit his white Mercedes which he was driving with the Clovelly club professional Maurice Bodmer at the Lakeside railway crossing having attended a lubricious celebration.

Little did I know the consequence of this strange turn of event would have on my life. No sooner had I got home than I struck a bargain with my friend Jonathan Bloch (I had been building a go-cart with some old pram wheels and I swapped these wheels for the clubs), for his late father's set of right-handed wooden shafted hickory golf clubs, thin white canvas bag, and old Dunlop 1,62mm golf balls.

Soon holes would appear in our garden with tins acting as golf holes, and for 15-minutes nightly on our Persian carpet in the lounge I was allowed to putt while listening to my serial, Mark Saxon, with his Russian side-kick, Sergei Grumolko (and his gun called Petruska).

At school I stole some wood from woodwork class, and built a raised hole to putt into, for which I got cuts, but I kept the wooden hole. An excellent contraption to utilise. Now I was the first person into the car on a Sunday afternoon as dad, dressed in his distinctive long white trousers, white shirt, and soft brown shoes, headed off to play bowls and I to play golf.

It was at this time that the first two Putt-Putt courses were built at Muizenberg beach which Bert van den Berg managed, and where I made sure I was the first paying customer, returning daily after school to practise as I started to earn myself a putting reputation after repeatedly watching Locke.

Once Locke even came to play scoring 29 (par is 36), but I held the course record for a time, including a score of 9 for nine holes.

By April I entered my first Junior tournament, the Western

To Barry
Best Wishes
Bobby Locke
1965

Province Prentice Open where I was brought down to earth shooting 168 and winning a golf ball for playing 'the most golf'. This was followed by the next event where I shot 142 and another golf ball. Not disillusioned by my astonishing scores I won my third tournament at Westlake, still playing right-handed with an unusual reverse grip and an incredible score of 100 *(I was later to shoot 32 on the second-nine at Clovelly and play off scratch)*.

Reflecting, I wonder how accurate me and my scorer's maths

played out that day? My handicap tumbled from 36 to 28, as I switched to playing left-handed being encouraged by Locke (I am naturally left-handed) whilst my lifetime friend, two-time LPGA major winner Sally Little, continued to play right-handed.

Later that year, and by now the putt-putt king of Muizenberg. I was now in regular competition with my Mouille Point rivals, Franklin and Hilton Stern as we somehow dominated the circuit against the adults. Who says youngsters have no nerves?

The golf body however warned me not to turn professional on the Putt-Putt circuit otherwise I would lose my golf amateur status and possible WP selection, whilst the Stern twins turned professional and benefited financially.

Meanwhile, Clovelly had decided to allow me and my best friend, Martin Gluck, to play in the club championship C Division, the first time that juniors were allowed to play. Our official handicaps were 28 and we had to drop them to 24 to play.

Round 1 and I shot a wonderful 90; in round 2 after going out in 50 I birdied the 18th for a 94, and I followed this up with two 92s winning by one shot, helped along by Locke's own caddy. What a thrill it was, with my dad walking the last nine holes.

My handicap was now cut to 18. That's a drop of 10 strokes in only two weeks. The beauty of being young. I was now alerted to the fact that the Western Province selectors of the junior team were watching my progress.

We also had a junior golf section where over 30 youngsters would meet daily during the school holidays.

My regular golf partners were Eric Casper, Marty Gluck, and later Moses Mooi. Soon I was playing for Clovelly as part of their top four Bradshaw Cup team.

By this time, I had befriended my golf hero, Locke, who would give me a lift home after he had finished playing his ukulele in the Clovelly pub and singing with the golfers while having a good time. Sometimes he would collect me to go watch him play in local professional tournaments.

Locke[12] was always encouraging me to go watch the 'better players', but I stuck with him, although he asked me not to talk to him while he was competing. After his round he would give me his numerous Dunlop 65 number 4 golf balls (four British Opens) with not a scratch on them, while at Clovelly he sometimes allowed me to play with him.

Strange how this rotund man could become my sporting hero given I was playing rugby and running cross-country for my school SACS. I would send him telegrams around the world whenever he posted a good score.

Soon I had made the semi-finals of the Under-15 WP Championships, and the following year at 15 I needed a par to make the top 8 at Metropolitan in the WP U19 championships playing with my beautiful friend the future two-time major winner on the LPGA, Sally Little[13], where after the first nine she was beating me. Oh, the embarrassment, the anguish. The following day I shot 76 with 22 putts, again with Sally. Now all I was dreaming about was a life as a professional golfer. Subsequently it was not to be as my law studies took precedent.

While living in Queensland years later, I proceeded my journey by playing in the Jack Newton Celebrity Pro-Am at Noosa, the second

---

12   In 2009 I would induct Locke into the Southern Africa Golf Hall of Fame.

13   **Sally Little** won 15 LPGA Tour events, including two majors during her career and was ranked 2nd in the world. In 2009, she became the first female golfer inducted into the Southern Africa Golf Hall of Fame.

of our Pro-Am (the first won by Ian Baker-Finch the future British Open champion) partnering Rodger Davis[14] on his way back into the world top 10 as he won the event beating Greg Norman, Ian Baker-Finch, Brett Ogle, Terry Price, Peter Senior, and Peter Fowler.

14　**Rodger Davis** won the PGA Tour of Australasia Order of Merit in 1990 and 1991. He made the top ten of the European Tour Order of Merit four times in the late 1980s and early 1990s. His seven European Tour wins included the British PGA Championship, and the Volvo Masters 1991. Davis was ranked in the top 10 of the Official World Golf Ranking for 29 weeks between 1987 and 1992. In the 1987 Open Championship he tied 2nd.

CHAPTER 3
CHELSEA RECORDS a world of music

For my 21st birthday my friends clubbed together, R5 each, to raise the R250 needed for a student flight to Europe. With my close friend Martin Gluck, we flew off to experience the world.

We arrived in Israel at the tail end of the Yom Kippur war. Although depressed it seemed such an exciting place to live. Very much 'live for today'. I was sure that would be the last war. Climbing down Masada, we bumped into our friends Johnny Kaplan and Norman Chorn climbing up.

There are many memories, and it wasn't long before we saw snow for the first time, and we were learning to ski at St. Anton, Austria where it was *bend ze neez unt shlide* from our instructor.

I had never seen a duvet before but there it was on my bed at the pension. I was sure it would fall off during the night with snow all around and that I would freeze. I carefully undid the duvet buttons and slid inside, but every morning the duvet was re-buttoned.

Madrid was fun as we had been joined by Norman and Johnny. That was until Marty brought back a young lady. We had agreed to all move into one side of our pension room with a drawn curtain.

Marty peeped through the curtain and whispered, *'They're all asleep,'* as angelic as we could, we pretended to sleep. Then Marty's bed began to squeak, and we couldn't hold back the laughter. The young lady screams, the door slammed, and Marty joined us. "You bastards," he said, laughing. Then it was off to Rome to see Santana, and we saw TV for the first time in London.

I ran out of money with three days to go, and would park myself at cafe tables the moment patrons left, and finish their meals. We flew back on my birthday, and the airline gave me an extra meal. I had lost seven kilos.

After highs and lows of my European trip, I returned to UCT. Playing for Law in the internal rugby league was very competitive, and some prominent players like Springbok Peter Whipp and Butch Deucher would sometimes join us. When we played at Coetzenberg against the Maties we grew wings and an extra yard in pace. We were sure that, from somewhere unseen in the stands, Danie Craven was watching for talent.

I was always getting injured, breaking this and that, and my nose bled copiously. Once, my friend Jane Trisos had to come onto the field to drag me off after I played on having broken my collarbone. Perhaps I thought I was another Jannie Engelbrecht, the Springbok who could play on with one arm. My best game was playing for SACS Old Boys 2nds with friends Trevor Zabow, Jonathan and Margo Pinshaw watching. My biggest surprise was when I finally realised I was actually too short, under five foot seven, and still be mixing it in the forwards.

Finally, after years of slog and toil, I reached my final year law, but no, I had failed a half-subject. You were not allowed to start final year until all your previous subjects had been passed. What was I to do?

I was at Newlands watching iconic cricketers Barry Richards (later to become a friend) and Graeme Pollock batting when there was an announcement calling me to the office where my cousin was waiting to take me to the airport to fly to Johannesburg.

I sensed the reason. My father had a heart-attack and passed while my folks were returning after visiting my sister and her family for three months in New Zealand. It occurred while flying over the Indian Ocean. Clearly help was limited.

Strangely, I received a letter from my dad three months later suggesting New Zealand should I ever wish to relocate. He reckoned they were a lot like Rhodesians where handshake deals meant something.

But now that part of my life was over. The answer came with a flight to Wellington, New Zealand, with money left to me by my great-aunt, and join my sister and brother-in-law Peters' hugely popular, Virgin type music megastore, Chelsea Records, which dominated the Wellington market with high turnover very low prices at its core. It was the talk of the town.

I flew to Wellington, in short pants and a light jersey. It was the middle of winter, but as the All Blacks came from New Zealand and played rugby and cricket, surely the weather was quite similar to Cape Town? It so happened we landed on the one and only sunny winters day, but boy was I in for a shock in Wellington where the radio station was called 'Radio Windy' (now *Radio Breeze*).

My sister's brother-in-laws, Ronny and David Jackson, were Maoris and it never occurred to me that they would be wary of me coming from apartheid South Africa. Fortunately it didn't take long for us to become firm friends. The fact that I was a white South African was never an issue to them, or at least that's what I hope. Soon Ronny and I were off to watch the All Blacks and a friendship with David developed such that he wanted to give me his All Black Olympic blazer.

Chelsea Records

Wellington's Chelsea Records was begun around 1974 by my brother-in-law Peter Bell and introduced an aggressive style of discounting previously found only in supermarkets. A popular local DJ with his own mobile disco (Sound Circus, with "fabulous lighting effects"), Peter had previously worked in London. (The shop he ran there was used in the film *A Clockwork Orange*, and he can be spotted near the front of the crowd in the film of the Rolling Stones' 1969 Hyde Park concert). With Richard Branson's innovative Virgin stores fresh in his mind, he set out to create his own hip music retail business. A large display wall would be deeply stocked with copies of the latest major releases, all bearing a discount sticker boasting "Their price/ Our price", the latter always being considerably cheaper.

*A flair for deep discounting: Peter Bell, founder of Chelsea
Records, Wellington, 1978*

Peter's original store was in Plimmer's Emporium on Plimmer's Steps, which also housed the trendy Toad Hall café and Printed Matter, Alister Taylor's underground bookshop. He borrowed $400 and Lindsay, my sister, ran the outlet while he operated a discotheque playing at Prime Minister 'Piggy' Muldoon's inauguration (he was later to be the narrator of the Rocky Horror Show), but his ambitions quickly outgrew the space. First, Peter moved to a narrow-fronted shop in Manners Mall, then to larger premises just a few doors away at 108 Manners St. This store's grand opening in 1978 saw him declaring it *"The largest record shop in New Zealand"* with *"over 80,000 albums in stock"*. By this time Chelsea also had a store at 209 Lambton Quay.

In 1979, in a bid to increase his buying power and discount opportunities, Peter decided to franchise the Chelsea brand. James Moss was Chelsea's first franchisee. After a decade in the cosmetics industry, Moss had worked briefly as a marketing manager for EMI before launching his own niche marketing company RCD (Record & Cassette Distributors Ltd.) His specialist stock included reggae, blues and children's music. One RCD-financed album *Carols for Christmas* sold 3,000 copies (LP and cassette). In cooperation with commercial broadcaster and children's entertainer Lindsay Yeo, RCD sold 10,000 albums by Yeo's alter-ego Buzz O'Bumble.

Meanwhile, The Music Shack was originally run by George Bell, Peter's brother in the Williams Centre, Plimmer's Lane, and ran from late 70s. Both this shop and Chelsea Records ran until well into the 90s, focusing on mainstream and Top 20 and, later, discounted CDs. Meanwhile Peter relocated initially to Sydney where he opened the Chelsea Records superstore in Pitt Street, the middle of the city dominating the Sydney inner music market with most of the original Wellington crew joining him, and also starting a video rental division

upstairs, before relocating to the Sunshine Coast where he started Rainbow Video franchise chain, and where I joined him. Later he was joined by George.

After meeting Lindsay in London, her and Peter had a spell in Cape Town which never really worked out. He was regarded as a bit of a bum by my mother. This was made worse by Lindsay's insistence that they were engaged, especially given that she was Jewish, and he Greek Orthodox. He set about converting to Judaism which satisfied the folks.

Although he worked in the records section of the Garlicks department store in the city and earned a salary, he was forbidden to stay in the same house as Lin. Instead, he lived in a crummy boarding house in Muizenberg, but had his meals and did his washing at our home. The final straw for the young couple was when Peter's work permit was rejected by the South African authorities and they

returned to New Zealand.

After their arrival in New Zealand, Peter borrowed $400 in order to start a record shore. At the same time, he operated a disco and became the leading DJ at night-time, whilst their shop, Chelsea Records, sold records at cost.

Lindsay and Peter's lock-wood Southgate Wellington home was situated on five-levels overlooking Cook Straight which the tourist buses referred to as *the glass house* because it had so many large thick windows (given the wind), and many music artists would come round, especially after concerts as Peter had his own recording studio. One of them was George Benson[15], and by 04:00, given

---

15 **George Benson** is a ten-time Grammy awards-winning American jazz musician and singer-songwriter.

that work commenced at 08:30, he was bundled out of the house. The best was Lin, who was besotted over Cliff Richard and being asked to have breakfast with him, was then so tongue-tied that she couldn't talk.

The first thing I was asked to do at Chelsea was to vacuum the floor. I had to go and ask one of the kids, how to turn it on, and then how to vacuum. So much for a law degree and my spoilt upbringing with a nanny. Memories of rain, with Chuck Mangione's *'Feel so good'* and Gerry Rafferty's *'Baker Street'* playing while it stormed outside come flooding back to me as I write this.

My reward was going skiing at Mount Ruapehu, and then by ferry between to South Island traversing the Cook Strait through the spectacular green rural islands comprising the Marlborough sounds, university town Christchurch with everyone riding bicycles, climbing Fox glacier, then skiing in beautiful Queenstown where the uncrowded slopes must be some of the best in the world, later a cable car to a restaurant up the mountain with the glittering fairy lights of the city below, the lake at Te Anau swimming amongst the snow in the hot water pools, and onwards all the way to the spectacular Milford Sound.

In Te Anu I met up with a young SA couple which was fun, and found a rare book, far away from source set in the early 1900s, *'Sally in Rhodesia'*, in a second-hand bookshop and which became useful in later life.

Cover of Kate Bush's album 'Kick Inside'

Another interesting meeting was with Kate Bush[16] who was only 19 and touring New Zealand with EMI promoting her *'Kick Inside'* album which songs she wrote, and which launched her to fame worldwide. She arrived at the Manners Plaza Chelsea Records, auburn hair and gorgeous looks. Lovely, slim, and friendly, although very short, which is why you never see her with another person in her promotional videos.

My sister came to me: *"EMI want to know if you would take Kate to dinner."* Traveling around the country she just needed time out. She

---

16 **'Kate' Bush** is an English singer, songwriter, record producer and dancer. In 1978 she topped the UK Singles Chart for four weeks with her debut single "Wuthering Heights". Bush has since released 25 UK Top 40 singles, including the Top 10 hits. All ten of her studio albums reached the UK Top 10. She was the first British solo female artist to top the UK album charts and the first female artist to enter the album chart at number one. Her debut album, The Kick Inside, was released in 1978.

was really sweet and pretty. However, she was not long in Wellington before heading on.

This, besides Locke, was possibly my first realisation as to how normal people are despite their fame, although I was already 26 so I shouldn't have felt intimidated.

Another interesting character I met was Euan Lloyd[17]. The famous film producer was giving an interview on the launch of his latest film, '*The Wild Geese*'. While being interviewed he was asked how he devised the film, and he said he was given the script by someone off the street. I asked him whether he would accept a script I had brought along. It went nowhere, of course, but unbeknownst to me, it was a start, an interest.

Upon my return to university to write my supp and for my final year, clearly, I couldn't do both law and art, so I put aside my art and focused on law. I graduated with my law degree and actually got good grades, which was absolutely amazing as I was the dumb ass at school, and every year the person below me failed. How can this be? It was not as if I enjoyed law, but of course I enjoyed playing rugby and the girls, even if I had become incredibly shy.

I had found it difficult to concentrate. It was many years later that I discovered I was Attention Deficit Disorder (ADD) which explained why my hands would not stop moving or scratching my head such that I had to wear a balaclava while studying and write everything down.

---

17   **Euan Lloyd** was a British film producer. His films included Paper Tiger, The Wild Geese, The Sea Wolves, and Who Dares Wins. His last film was Wild Geese II.

CHAPTER 4

The LAW or AUSTRALIA

At around about this time, I received a call from my sister Lindsay in Sydney to inform me that my mom, who was visiting relatives, Pat and Vicky Sino in Melbourne, had fallen out of a moving tram, was in a coma, and not expected to live. I was told to hurry across to Australia as soon as possible.

I hopped onto a flight to Johannesburg and then a Qantas/SAA flight to Sydney, and from there to Melbourne. The Sinos met me at the airport, and took me to see my mom. Apparently the tram had jerked forward and mom, who was standing at the entrance area, simply went flying off.

Many years previously mum had had a life-threatening operation which required some of her skull to be cut away. The operation was successful, but meant her skull in the operated-upon area was thin. This was the part of her head on which she landed in her fall off the Melbourne tram and, because her skull wasn't adequate protection for her brain, she had landed up in a coma.

By then Lindsay and Peter, who was now *New Zealand Young Businessman of the Year'* had relocated to Sydney, initially to Mossman, and then Manly, and had this time taken the Sydney music world by storm having set up Chelsea Records in the heart of the city, where Chelsea's sales were now so legendary such that police had to monitor the crowd.

While I was at the Melbourne Royal Hospital, mom emerged from the coma, but her left side was paralysed. My sister having chartered a small plane to get her to Melbourne now informed me that she would not be able to care for her. I think this was a way of trying to get me to stay in Australia, so I had choices to make.

The Sinos were simply brilliant and funny and I so enjoyed staying with them and traveling to their work. They were furriers in downtown Melbourne. Fur coats and luscious young girl assistants. I thought I was in heaven. Vicky was especially funny painting her face black to make me feel at home. (*I know that may sound racist, but it was funny.*)

I simply took this all for granted and never questioned the future. This continued for six weeks as mom recovered. I also spent a lot of time with their two daughters, Elizabeth married to Michael, and Barbara married to Henry Wasserman with their baby. One night I accompanied Henry on an Avis truck drive to Sydney. Along the way we stopped at a truck restaurant in the middle of the night. I felt special hanging out with the trucky crowd.

Michael had a solicitor friend who took on mom's case, as she now faced 9 months of rehabilitation hospitals, and he then offered me law articles. What an opportunity! I wonder what I would have done were my father alive to advise me? Meanwhile I went on a dinner date with my mom's nurse, Annette Perry. Looking back, it was possibly my most romantic date.

People's memory of Chelsea

The last record store that I can remember was a place called Chelsea Records which was like a combination of a JB store and one of those $10 CD stores that were around a few years ago. In the early 80's they used to buy album box sets in bulk, break them up and sell the records individually at bargain

prices. I got so many Beatle albums for about 4 or 5 bucks each which was like half price (albums were generally $8.99 or $9.99 then). And something that seems funny to me now was, I discovered that in the back lane behind the store they would dump all the empty box set boxes and so one day I got my dad to drive in and we took a bunch of these boxes home! Loads of them! Beatles, Stones, Lennon. Why? It just seemed cool having all these record boxes in my room! And I still have the Stones one that my parents ended up keeping their Scrabble pieces in!

They were exciting days as those stores were like a window into another world and pretty much the only way to find anything that wasn't completely mainstream. How things have changed…

I reach back to the early 80's when Chelsea records down past Martin Pl in Pitt Street was operating. Open 7 days had a lot of close outs and great range of punk, new wave, ska, along with pop and regular top 40 stuff. Crammed full of stock, it was one on my Sunday morning haunts as a kid when only a

Chelsea Records in Pitt Street, Sydney on August 24, 1982.

*few record stores and bookshops were open in a pretty much deserted city centre.
I felt like the city was my own as I wandered from shop to shop on a Sunday
morning. It was my secret world, no one I knew, knew about.*

*"Chelsea Records" I think was next on the corner of King and Pitt Streets
(across the road from the Tank Stream Arcade entrance). I had always wondered
why I was able to pick up lots of rare New Zealand second hand singles at
this shop when, just a few hours ago when doing some research on the net, I
discovered the owner was a Kiwi! They didn't last long (early/mid 80's?). Lots
of bargains and it would be packed at lunchtimes.*

Peter Bell's story

Peter was a brilliant salesman with big original ideas who knew how
to market, and his music knowledge was first rate.

He was brought up by his grandmother in New Zealand, and left
school at 15. After meeting Lindsay in London, they both arrived in

Cape Town and tried to impress the family, but Peter was regarded as a bit of a bum. This was made worse by Lindsay's insistence that they were engaged given that she was Jewish, and he Greek Orthodox. He wasn't allowed to stay in the same house as Lin, so he lived in a crummy boarding house in Muizenberg, but had his meals and washing at our home, while he worked with records at Garlicks departmental store in the city. Returning on a visit from the army, I gave them both a good welcome before returning to barracks.

I was to meet up with him and my sister Lindsay in London in January 1974 and again in Sydney where I later went to work for him. We went shopping and entered a posh clothing store. Peter was dressed in old tatty clothes and none of the shop attendants bothered to serve him, that was until he flashed a large wad of notes. It was like honey to bees. I helped carry the numerous shopping bags back to the hotel.

In Sydney I started off staying in my friend's Dee Why apartment while they went off on holiday. I would get up a 5:30 am run down to the beach for a swim, catch a bus for an hour ride to the city at 06:45 am, have a coffee and start work at 08:30. Work through until 4 pm, then catch a bus to see my mom in hospital. Then another bus at 19:45 pm eventually getting home at 21:00 pm and supper. It was hard, but the only way.

No sooner was I working with Peter in Sydney than John Lennon was assassinated on December 8, 1981. Peter placed a wreath in the window which caught the attention of national television, and now we were appearing on the national news. John Lennon was possibly one of the greatest talents, not just his music but his views on life.

In South Africa the Beatles were banned. The irony was that Lennon would visit Cape Town and went unrecognised.

Chelsea Records was the iconic music place in Sydney as Peter also controlled and took bookings for the DJs and was the darling of the music companies such that TDK chairman visited from Japan and gave Peter an award for selling the most blank cassettes. Likewise he received a number of framed gold records for sales, whilst we were invited to special private performances by various artists like Jon English[18] and Marc Hunter[19], which were amazing.

Friends were visiting on a "look see" relocation, so we decided to go on a holiday to Airlie Beach. Little did I know this would one day be my home.

What a fun town for backpackers, like Torremolinos[20] during the 1960s in Spain, being the gateway to the Barrier Reef, before Hayman, Hamilton, and South Molle islands were developed. Soon Jonathan Pinshaw, Barry Friedman, Bobby Heilbrun, Robert Lipman, and me were sailing on Gretel the 1962 Americas Cup Challenger, then Kaizer Matanzima's (Transkei PM) yacht Solo, watching toad racing, playing golf, and swimming in the humid resort pool at midnight.

Most of those who worked for Chelsea Records in Wellington

---

18 **Jon English** was an Australian singer, songwriter, musician and actor. He took on the role of Judas Iscariot in the Australian version of the stage musical Jesus Christ Superstar from May 1972; his Australian top twenty hit singles include "Turn the Page", "Hollywood Seven", "Words are Not Enough", "Six Ribbons" and "Hot Town", and was acclaimed for his starring role in the 1978 Australian TV series Against the Wind.

19 **Marc Hunter** was a New Zealand rock and pop singer, songwriter and record producer. He was the lead vocalist of Dragon. He was also a member of the Party Boys in 1985. For his solo career he issued five studio albums

20 One of the most popular novels to be set in Spain is James A Michener's Drifters, part of which is set in Torremolinos. The bestseller is a powerful drama based on the lives of six young runaways adrift in a world of drugs, dreams and pleasure.

Jonathan Pinshaw, Bobby Heilbrun, Barry Cohen Airlie Beach 1980

came over to Sydney, and we were one big happy family. What a great time, catching a ferry from Manly and later Mossman in the morning to work as yachts sailed by, a cup of coffee, learning and working with people much more knowledgeable about music, with Peter buying records in bulk and selling them really cheap.

Peter based the operation on high turnover low prices, and we would go to the EMI warehouse and buy deleted copies for $500,000, then sell then for $1-4 including the Beatle albums. I was once again working with Eric Morris, David (who named me 'Daktari' after a favourite African tv programme) and Ronny Jackson[21], Graeme Regan (with whom I initially shared digs), Peter's sisters Stella, Anna,

NewZealand Olympian David Jackson 1978

---

21 **Ronny and David Jackson** boxed for NZ in the Commonwealth Games, training with Muhammed Ali and his trainer Bundini Brown, David also boxed in the 1978 Olympics whilst Ronny played for the Maori rugby team, and later both boys played Australia Senior 7s national rugby team.

and Helen, and even his estranged father joined for a while from Greece.

Peter also had an older DJ friend, Ken working there. He was gay, and this was the first time I had interacted with a male who was different from me. At first I steered well clear of him, but once I got over the surprise and that he wasn't going to hit on me, I realised we were all the same.

The weeks leading up to Christmas in December were an incredibly busy time. We were selling thousands of records, and the police had to control the crowds trying to get into the store. At this time I was now staying with my school friend, Robert Lipman, a budding accountant at Bondi Junction.

Christmas Eve, what a night, money flowing like wine, such that we drank our way through serving. Inside was air conditioned, but outside warm and muggy. Then leaving the store, around 21:30 pm I was hit by the warm humid air and when I stepped outside and walked to Martin Place to catch the underground tube to Bondi Junction, I simply keeled over and ended up *kotching* (vomiting) twelve times when conscious, and I recall someone asking if I was okay, which of course I responded positively.

By the time I got down to the underground, the trains were no longer running, so I hailed a taxi. The problem was I never knew the address only the way I would walk from the station. Driving to Bondi Junction sitting in the front of the cab, I was steering a make-believe steering-wheel in tandem with the taxi driver, and in my stupor retraced my steps back to my friend's apartment. Somehow we got there.

After six weeks my friend went to Cape Town for two weeks, hooked up with a Muizenberg girl, Susan Smith, and returned a married man, which was not only a massive surprise but meant I had to pack up and leave quickly.

Fortunately I was able to share digs in Bondi with my other best school friend, Trevor Zabow, a solicitor, and his young son, who was still a baby. I had introduced him to his wife, Shelly Bartlett[22] but this marriage had not worked out, so Trev and I took turns to babysit while the other went out on a date. It was a real learning experience for the future.

Bondi was fun in those days, although I was disappointed in the beach which was so famous and purported to be amongst the best in the world. Certainly Muizenberg was better, and there are many others I have experienced over the years. Later, night-time going to acting classes at the Australian Film & Television school, and enjoying the Sydney night-life.

The first red flag concerning Peter was when he got into an altercation with Eric Morris who did not agree with a decision Peter was making. Eric had followed Peter to Sydney from Wellington at Peter's request, and managed the store when Peter was not available. To our shock, Peter fired him on the spot. Loyalty out of the window, but then I grudgingly accepted it because I was in awe of Peter, I idolised him. I guess the others felt the same way, anyway we didn't want to make waves in case we lost our jobs.

By now, Mom had to learn to walk, talk, and eat again. She was unable to use her left hand which remained paralysed. This was a slow painful nine month experience in hospital in a strange country. Her only visitors being me, Lindsay, Peter, and her grandchildren Mandi and Sasha.

I never really thought about how difficult this was for her. One

---

22 Her sister and my friend, Jenny Bartlett, married the famous singer, the 'white Zulu', Johnny Clegg.

moment she was touring the world, the next in hospital. Her previous and only other overseas trip had seen my dad pass on while they were in the air over the Indian Ocean returning from New Zealand.

As mentioned I had been working in the music industry so when two elderly ladies approached me during a flight and asked if I worked in records, I replied in the affirmative, wondering how they knew. Then *"Are you Paul McCarthy of the Beatles?"* one of them asked. I couldn't help myself and smiled.

Nine-months later towards of the end of the year it was time to leave Chelsea Records and take mom back to Cape Town. My sister had booked us first class, the only time I have ever travelled first class. Raymond Ackerman[23] was also travelling first class, and we spent time having a nice chat. Our paths continued to cross over the years.

I hadn't studied for nothing, so now it was back to Cape Town to do my two-year law articles. What a bore! The best part was going to court, pretending I was already admitted, and appearing for clients, then ducking out to see a movie.

Meanwhile with Chelsea's lease terminating, and given that the Sydney lifestyle was not for my sister having grown up in a small seaside town, she gave her husband Peter an ultimatum. *"I'm going to the Sunshine Coast with the two kids, somewhere we can amble down to the*

23　**Raymond Ackerman** won the Outstanding Young South African award in 1965, and at the age of 35 he was the managing director of 85 Checkers stores; however, he was fired in the same year. In response, Ackerman bought four stores in Cape Town trading under the name Pick 'n Pay. Under his leadership, Pick 'n Pay eventually grew into one of Africa's largest supermarket chains, with a thirty-seven billion Rand turnover (2006 figure) and more than 124 supermarkets, 14 hypermarkets and 179 franchised outlets. The Pick 'n Pay Group employs more than 30,000 people in several African countries. He also was chairman and owned Clovelly Country Club, which he gave to the members.

beach with a bucket and spade. You can come or continue here at Chelsea."

Actually my first job was with Readers Digest as their assistant product manager book division where we launched the legendary Illustrated Guide to South Africa (IGSA) and Southern Africa Land of Beauty and Splendour (SALOBS). I was working under an attractive older lady Ms. Bentley who was under a lot of pressure and too busy to delegate or train me. It was a very statistic orientated job of databases to focus mailout marketing and was very much in the marketing mix, which I found quite daunting. Nevertheless, I was treated very well by Brian Barends, the CEO, although my work was relegated to simply cutting, recording and pasting. On a Friday afternoon we all got together in the boardroom for sandwiches and a drink. Apparently everyone was satisfied with my performance.

After around six months, on the spur of the moment, when a fellow I worked with gave his notice to become a pilot, I decided to leave as well as I felt I wasn't learning anything. Quite frankly it was a really stupid decision as this was an international company with potential for travel. I just didn't understand and should've had someone to talk it through with, but those were the cards that I dealt.

Time to join a law firm, given that was what I had studied for. I was initially flown to Pretoria for an interview with Adams & Adams the copyright patent and trademark specialist. This was right up my ally. They offered me the job at R900 per month, which was just enough to survive on. However when I walked outside there were security people walking around their building with machine guns, and given the perception that Pretoria was the bastion of Afrikanerdom, I turned down the offer.

Stubborn is an understatement; copyright, patent, and trademark was exactly what I wanted to do, and here I was being offered the opportunity at the most prestigious of law firms. Unfortunately, my prejudice against Afrikaner folk following my army experiences simply got in the way.

I was delighted when I was offered articles at the prestigious C&A Friedlander law firm, one of the big four in Cape Town, at only R300 per month, which was not enough to survive on. Clearly they were banking on my bringing in clients through my golfing reputation. I saw this as a road to wealth and success. My uncle was well known to them as it had a substantial Jewish clientele. I simply expected I would go to the top. I didn't question how I should be working extra hard or pushing my way forward. I naively expected success.

But then most of those doing law either entered the profession or proceeded down the financial company route. I simply had blinkers. Even at C&A, as stupid as it may sound, I was unaware that I, and not the law firm, was supposed to register for law articles or that I was required to go after-hours for a six month article course before I wrote the board exam.

In order to reduce my expenses I bummed accommodation at my friend, Michael Allen, who had a cottage in Sea Point. Next door was his cousin Tamara Saacks whom I asked out on a date. Little did I know our paths would continually cross and a real friendship develop over the years. Later I shared accommodation in a really fun house in London Road with Barry and Vicky Zworenstine, his brother Mark and Richard Rom. Many a night we would stay up talking, listening to music, playing the guitar, and occasionally going to the beachfront to watch the sun rise.

I still harboured ambitions of playing golf at a professional level, but repeated attempts at provincial amateur opens where I was competing against guys like future world star and friend David

Frost[24], and the lack of time to practice convinced me I did not have the temperament. Nor did I hit the ball far enough to compete at that level despite the fact that I was a brilliant putter. Meanwhile my friend Sally Little was making huge waves on the LPGA tour in the USA.

Should I have become a club professional? Yet again I thought, given my hard studies, that this was beneath me, yet passion eventually always pushes through and so it was proved to be.

So here I was in a small law office with a stack of files in front of me. You know, the files that no one wants, which all seemed to come my way. Small debt collection, divorces, litigation, summons's, and court appearances.

My office was next door to that of the former mayor, Dicky Friedlander, while to my left was councillor Bertie Sterne's office. Bertie had formed the Muizenberg scouting movement with my dad, was one of the founders of False Bay Rugby Club, and the founder of the Masque Theatre. He was one of Muizenberg's true identities, a wonderful citizen, who lived on the Muizenberg beach front.

Life's twists and turns. You plan to go left, and you end up going right. I had just returned from appearing in the magistrates court, something I was not allowed to do as I had only completed 19 months of my two-year law articles, but if you don't tell, nor will I.

Lindsay called from Australia to say her and Peter had a video store for me to manage, which would also allow me to play a little golf, so to come over immediately and bring mom so we could be

---

24 **David Frost** was ranked in the top 10 of the Official World Golf Ranking in the late 1980s and early 1990s. Frost has 29 professional tournament wins to his name, including the World Series of Golf, South African Open, Nedbank Million Dollar Challenge and Canadian Open. He has also been on the winning Alfred Dunhill Cup team and played in the Presidents Cup.

a family again. I agreed to take mom and have a look see.

I immediately informed Frank Muggleston under whom I was doing articles and was granted a two-week leave of absence, packed for 2-3 weeks, and immediately flew to Australia. Quite frankly I was delighted to get away from the repetitive grind of being an articled clerk. But being close to my mom, I had other things on my mind.

Now I had to also make a decision.

CHAPTER 5
RAINBOW VIDEO & Airlie Beach

I informed Frank Muggleston I would not be able to return to complete my articles, despite my uncle Lionel doing everything to try and persuade me to change my mind. Lionel was looking to the future, opportunity and security, while I was only in the here and now. Another crossroad.

So off to Maroochydore where Peter had opened Rainbow Video which I was to take over and another store in Caloundra which he would run. The idea was that I would have a half share in the head office, I could play much more golf, and we could be a family again.

Mom, Maria, the family domestic helper, and I arrived at our wonderful accommodation at Cotton Tree in Maroochydore overlooking the beach in warm sub-tropical weather. Heaven had come. For Maria this was a shock from apartheid South Africa, where as a mixed race lady she was regarded as a second-class citizen. Here everyone was friendly towards her, even more so when they heard she was from South Africa. At Church she was treated as a celebrity.

So I 'jumped ship' from a promising law career, and took over the video store Peter had opened half way along the Main Road of Maroochydore. It was a relatively small store of around 80 sm. with substantial signage outside. Peter was charging me 35% interest on the money he was loaning me. I trusted him implicitly, and did not query the usury interest rate which turned out to be illegal in Australia.

Barry with Maria in Australia 1983

What was I thinking? I soon employed two surfer dudes, Vernon (Ernie) Underwood and Dieter Johnson who were living on the dole in a house with two others and spending the day surfing. Ernie arrived in boardshorts and a beanie. I sent him home to change. We were to have a great time together and we are still friends to this day. Peter also sent Sharon Withford to help manage the store.

It wasn't long before I joined the Nambour Rugby Club in the rough inland town closeby. After about five minutes during my first practise an elbow went into my mouth as I spat out my front tooth.

I have broken many bones playing rugby, but never my teeth, and I thought this was as good a time as any to 'retire'. I simply walked off the field never to play again. It was time to play squash...*squash the couch.*

'The Race of the Century'

Soon after arriving in Queensland we experienced the true Aussie never say die spirit. We were fortunate to watch the greatest yacht race ever, the Americas Cup!

Coming from isolated South Africa I didn't know that much about the America's Cup, other than after 132 years, America always won. Now we were glued to the television early every morning until close to 10:00.

It was amazing, and before this, I would have said yacht racing was boring, but the more you watched the more you began to appreciate the tactics, wind shits, and seamanship. It was Australia, a small country of 17 million, the David vs. Goliath, the might of America supertech, and hugely expensive aeronautic boats.

The 1983 America's Cup was a 12-metre class yacht racing series which pitted the defending New York Yacht Club's Liberty against the Royal Perth Yacht Club's challenger, Australia II.

Liberty won all the Defender trials. The challenger was Australia II and they were competing for the Louis Vuitton Cup.

Alan Bond arrived at Newport with Australia II, billed as one of the biggest threats to American dominance of the 12 Metre class. The boat was designed by Ben Lexcen and skippered by John Bertrand. The revolutionary "winged keel" of the Australian yacht was a subject of controversy from the outset of the challenger series, with the New York Yacht club alleging that the winged keel boat was not a legal 12-Metre, and that the keel design itself was the result of Dutch engineers, and not by Lexcen. This second point could have made Australia II illegal under the requirement that the boat be "designed and constructed in country" as the Deed of Gift that governed the competition stipulated. The boat was ruled a legal 12 Metre, and she was allowed to participate in the regatta. The speed of the new contender, along with the controversy and protests intensified international media attention to the series.

Whilst it is always the aim to have the best sails, best design and best crew for maximum boat speed, yacht racing is also about tactical manoeuvres and reading the wind on the course. Choosing when to change direction, called 'tacking' upwind or 'gybing' downwind under spinnaker, can make significant gains or losses regardless of how good the yacht is. Australia II dominated the challenger series and entered the America's Cup finals as the most promising contender to date.

We knew Australia II was faster than Liberty, but the U.S. yacht won the first and second races by margins of more than a minute when the Australian yacht suffered equipment failure, but the Australia II took the third race, then Liberty won the fourth. This meant Liberty had only to win one more race, whilst Australia II had to win the next three races.

By then the Aussie crew had adopted Men at Work's song *"Down Under"* as its theme song. It is ultimately about celebrating the country.

The lyrics to "Down Under" depict an Australian man travelling the globe, meeting people who are interested in his home country. Slang and drug terms were featured in the lyric, and "full of zombie" refers to the use of a type of marijuana. The song also contains the refrain "where beer does flow and men "chunder" (vomit).

Despite the optimism it seemed like a bridge too far, and the Americans were ready to celebrate another victory. Back came Australia II to win the fifth and sixth races. This was the first time the America's Cup had needed a sixth race, let alone a seventh.

The cup title came down to the seventh and final race. The San Diego Yacht Club did everything to have the Australia boat expelled, they even sent frogmen to photograph the mysterious 'winged keel' which had been kept under wraps draped with a curtain. But the frogman were caught, and the cry went up, CHEATS!

For the seventh and deciding race on 26 September 1983 the wind was light at around eight knots. The pre-start was not a typical match race start. "Neither party wanted to make a mistake and end up in the protest room," Conner would explain later. Liberty won the start by eight seconds ahead of Australia II on paper but the Australians held a controlling position at the favoured end sailing toward the favoured side which gave them the early lead. Australia II was subsequently overtaken by Conner who built up what seemed to be an unassailable margin. At the start of the penultimate leg (a square run) the America's Cup looked like it would stay in Newport.

Conner failed to cover Australia II which allowed them to run deeper and faster assisted by breeze and windshifts allowing Australia II to overtake the Americans by the leeward mark. Conner then engaged Australia II in a spectacular tacking duel with nearly 50 tacks including a number of faked "dummy" tacks trying to break the Australians' cover. Australia II held on until both boats reached the starboard layline in amongst the spectator fleet and tacked several boat lengths ahead of Liberty and sailed to the finish to take the race. Australia II crossed the finish line with a winning margin of 41 seconds, becoming the first successful challenger in the 132 years "since the schooner America won it in a race around England's Isle of Wight in 1851".

The final race was televised in Australia in the early hours just before dawn, and the victory was celebrated in public venues across Australia. Prime Minister Bob Hawke was interviewed at the dawn celebration at Royal Perth Yacht Club, Western Australia. To rapturous laughter and applause, he said with finality: *"Any boss who sacks a worker for not turning up today is a bum"*.

It was almost like a fossil event – it was created before there was such a thing as international sport, it predates cricket, it certainly predates the modern Olympics, and yet one nation had always won it.

The campaign saw the debut of the now iconic Boxing Kangaroo flag. Australia II was Alan Bond's fourth attempt at winning.

For Australia II Ben Lexcen devised a revolutionary winged keel.

There was international sort of publicity about this funny-looking keel. All the sailors around the world, but particularly the USA, desperately wanted to see what it was like, and there was talk about how they were going to unveil it, have a bit of fun to make a big deal of the publicity of it, and Bond[25] said to them *'no, let's not do it at all, let's just hide it and keep it hidden'*.

America was the leading technological nation in the world and now here was little Australia popping up with Ben Lexcen's new technology.

Australia called a layday, then the wind was too light to sail, then the Americans called a layday. Now everyone was on tenterhooks, nerves stretched including the viewing public.

When the gun finally fired on 26 September, two edgy teams, fully aware of the intense interest and outcome, got away to a tame start with Australia II in the slightly better position.

As the two boats began tacking up the course, Australia II realised they faced a much faster Liberty and had lost some advantage they had previously held in these light shifty conditions. Shifty was a key word – the breeze had small, but important variations in direction and strength, and Liberty was first to gain, edging out ahead by just a couple of boat lengths when it benefited from a better patch of breeze part way up the leg. They rounded the first mark with this small advantage, kept it on the first reach, and then lost ground on the next leg as Australia II nearly caught up again, showing it could

---

25 **Alan Bond** bankrolled the successful challenge for the 1983 America's Cup which resulted in his selection s Australian of the Year. That victory is widely regarded as one of Australia's greatest international sporting achievements. He was noted for his high-profile and corrupt business dealings, including his central role in the WA Inc scandals of the 1980s, what was at the time the biggest corporate collapse in Australian history and also his criminal conviction in 1997 that saw him serve four years in prison.

do well under spinnaker on a square run – in hindsight this was a warning of things to come. They were still in the race and niggled away up the next windward leg, but just as Australia II closed on Liberty, another shift in direction and strength went Liberty's way and they pulled out to almost a minute lead, turning into the next square run.

One last leg to try and catch Liberty but we were too far behind. No one caught up a minute on the last leg. We were going to lose, or were we?

This was where everything Australia II had done came to the fore. Sensing the breeze was stronger on the left they followed Liberty toward that side, and they immediately began to close the gap. Liberty then gybed to try and cover Australia II, who held their nerve and stayed with the better breeze while Liberty sailed into a lighter patch.

All the way down the course Australia II's crew held their composure. When they did gybe they chose the right moments to take advantage of the small wind changes, while Liberty was losing more ground with additional gybes at the wrong moment, trying the keep in touch with Australia II as it gained on them.

The Australian television viewers were urging and cheering the boat along as it gained on Liberty, from depression to euphoria. Here we come! Australia II was dictating the tactics now from behind, and eventually they drew parallel, but going both faster and lower, meaning they were covering less ground toward the next mark.

As they closed on the last rounding mark at the bottom of the course, with both boats on opposing gybes the moment came when Australia II passed ahead of Liberty, still sailing faster and in phase with the small wind shifts.

Choosing the right timing Australia II gybed down and then back again to the mark, rounding 21 seconds ahead of a horrified US team on Liberty.

We had them and the Americas Cup was coming to Australia, or was it...

Liberty gained, but could not get even and neither team made any mistakes with their crew work despite making well over 40 tacks. Approaching the finish Conner tried one last trick, taking the yachts out to one side, beyond the shortest course to the finish, trying to gain time and maybe a wind shift that would close the gap. In the end it was Australia II that got a slight advantage when they tacked back toward the finish line, still holding a slim lead.

Australia II benefited from a stronger gust and pulled away from Liberty, crossing 41 seconds ahead, and into a permanent place in sporting history.

Australia II came home to a hero's welcome in Newport the likes of which this historic seaport has never seen. And the secret winged keel revealed. It was a wonderful, once-in-a-lifetime moment, and Bondy clearly loved every minute of it, and so did we as we celebrated through the day and night.[26]

Back at Rainbow Video we were very busy as our policy was to buy multiple copies of the top releases which we returned for a rebate after three and six weeks, or three months. My opposition, Sunseeker, was further down the road. He had a large store but we had the edge due to my marketing and our friendliness. We were also open for 24-hours and I regularly pulled the graveyard shift.

David and Helen, as well as Ronny and Stella were staying down

26   1987 Denis Conners won back the Americas Cup from the Australians.

the road opposite the surfing beach at Alexander Headlands and were working for Peter at Coloundra, whilst Helen was at my new store in Mooloolaba. While not working they were in the water surfing with legends 'Kong' Elkington and Les Purcell (who was later to become my partner at Airlie Beach).

When Sharon left to join Peter's operation doing his bookkeeping, Grant McQuarrie joined me. By this stage I was living in an apartment opposite the sea at Alexandra Headlands, with a swimming pool and where we would get together. The whole family was here. The beaches were fantastic, the water warm.

It did not take long before Peter was approached for franchises, and I was his right-hand opening various stores.

Soon we were branding our cars 'Rainbow Video' and franchising stores along the Sunshine Coast. Stores at Noosa, Gympie, Coolum, Nambour, Mooloolaba, in addition to Maroochydore and Caloundra as we took over the Sunshine Coast with 14 outlets.

My function was to oversee the building of the layout and getting these stores ready to open. In return, I was to have a shareholding in the head office.

It was at this time that I also attended the opening of Pick 'n Pay's superstore on the outskirt of Brisbane to be run by my friend's brother and SACS old boy, David Goldberg. Raymond Ackerman, Pick 'n Pay's founder opened the store and we all received heavy gold plated paperweights. But it was not to be, as the trade unions turned against this South African operation given their opposition to the apartheid policies.

A few months after arriving, Liane Drew (23) and her mother entered the store still in their gym workout outfit. She immediately caught my attention and it wasn't long before we were regularly dating. Everything seemed wonderful, but like everything, life has a way of providing twists.

Jack Newton Celebrity Pro-Am

Golf raised its head again when I was invited in 1983 to participate in this Jack Newton Celebrity Pro-Am.

As the end of season event for the professional golfers every major Australian golfer was participating from Greg Norman in short pants, Ian Baker-Finch on his way to winning The Open, Brett Ogle, Peter Senior, Rodger Davis and even Jack Newton. Who had recently lost an eye and arm in a propeller accident, participating, one-handed.

The Jack Newton Celebrity Pro-Am golf event was to become an annual held in December 1983 at the Tewantin Noosa Golf Club in aid of junior golf along with programs with indigenous and disabled young people.

It was believed that professional golfers would enjoy a post-season Pro-Am and to add to the tournament the Club would also invite celebrities, entertainers and sports people to play.

The event had a great 'feel' about it, especially to propagate a Celebrity type event. From Prime Ministers to Olympic Champions, movie stars to comedians and footballers to entrepreneurs, they were all part of the Celebrity family who gathered annually for two days. The Celebrity stories and the general banter were incredible.

Sadly, the world did not see Jack's true potential during the height of his professional career. He had a near-fatal accident in July 1983 when he walked into the spinning propeller of a Cessna aeroplane he was about to board at Sydney Airport. He ultimately survived the accident, losing an eye and an arm, and this Pro-Am in December was held in his honour.

Jack Newton after his accident   *Liane Drew*

Our four-ball consisted of Dave Fordham[27], the legendary Rugby commentator, Jack Gibson[28] the guru and former coach of Australian Rugby League, and Rodger Davis[29] who was making a comeback following his partner's theft of their Buderim hotel property investment and who later would be elevated into one of the world's top ten golfers.

Being rather ignorant and new concerning Rugby League I turned

---

27 **David Fordham**, sports journalist, become a worldwide household name in sport covering three rugby union world cups, countless rugby union Tests, as well as numerous contests in cricket, golf, tennis, rugby league and many a Kangaroo tour, as well as four Olympics & Commonwealth Games for channels Ten and Seven.

28 **Jack Gibson** was an Australian rugby league coach, player, and commentator. He is widely considered one of the greatest coaches in the sport's history. Nicknamed 'Supercoach', he was highly regarded not only for his coaching record but also for his thirst for innovation as he introduced new coaching and training methods into the sport in the 1970s and 1980s.

29 **Rodger Davis** won the PGA Tour of Australasia Order of Merit in 1990 and 1991. He made the top ten of the European Tour Order of Merit four times. His seven European Tour wins included the British PGA Championship, and the Volvo Masters. He was ranked in the top 10 of the Official World Golf Ranking for 29 weeks. In the 1987 Open Championship, he tied for 2nd place.

to Gibbo and asked him *"What do you do"*. Oh boy, I felt like such a complete idiot and clammed up thereafter.

Playing behind us was Bob Hawke in shorts with his boney legs, the newly elected Prime Minister of Australia, and *Aussie* Joe Bugner[30] who had fought Muhammed Ali for the World Heavyweight title, and who despite his tree-trunk arms and no neck, struggled to hit the ball more than 100 metres. Playing in the four-ball in front of us was the '(in)famous' Minister of the Environment Barry Cohen (who had sex with his wife on his office desk) enquiring whether I was also Jewish – jeepers, with a name like 'Cohen'.

At the same time, I was aware that the Australian Governor-General, Sir Ninian Stephen seemed to me to be taking a more than healthy interest in Liane, whilst down the fairway we spied a girl sitting right in the middle of where we were teeing-off, oblivious to us golfers, playing with the butterflies dreamily. We shouted at her a number of times, but to no available until finally it dawned on her. How could I tell them that this was my sister?

At the end of the round with Rodger Davis finally winning the event, we were surrounded by young autograph hunters (there was a large crowd of spectators at the event), reminding me of my early days. First, they poured around Rodger, well he had just won the event, then famous Gibbo and Dave Fordham. I was wearing an 'Out of Africa' (starring Robert Redford and Meryl Streep – Karen

---

30   **'Joe' Bugner** is a former heavyweight boxer and actor. He unsuccessfully challenged Muhammad Ali for the heavyweight championship in 1975. Bugner twice held the British and British Commonwealth heavyweight titles and was a three-time European heavyweight champion. He was ranked among the world's top ten heavyweights in the 1970s, fighting such opponents as Ali, Joe Frazier, Jimmy Ellis, and Henry Cooper, retiring from boxing after a TKO loss to Frank Bruno in 1987. He made a final comeback winning the lightly regarded World Boxing Federation (WBF) heavyweight championship in 1998 at the age of 48 against James "Bonecrusher" Smith.

Blixen *"I had a farm in Afrika"*, which farm today is the premier golf course in Kenya, the Karen Golf Club) sweatshirt which the film distributor had given me. Anyway, after these youngsters had their autographs, one of them blurted out, pointing at me, that he had seen me in Out of Africa and I was flooded with requests for my autograph. A bucket list tick, to be asked for my autograph, my moment in the sun.

Towards the end of 1983 Maria was getting homesick and decided she wanted to return to Cape Town to be with her family. She and mom had now become best friends and this was very hard for both of them. Of course Maria was also my 'other mum', and we were sad to see her go.

In late 1984 I sold my Maroochydore outlet for $150,000, part cash part townhouse in Peregian, Noosa Shire, right opposite the beach. It was a wonderful townhouse on three levels and a complex swimming pool outside. Bottom level was accommodation for Martine and model Jessica Allen who stayed with me while holidaying, with Jessica now dating Dieter.

Peregian beach was long and relatively empty. The water was warm, although there was a relatively strong side-current. At night I would take a deck chair and sit on the beach under the gazillion stars just like Jane Fonda and Jason Robards did in the film 'Julia' while the waves crashed in front of me. But it wasn't long before Peter was pressuring me to sell the townhouse and repay his loan so he could use the money to expand the operation.

Now I bought the most wonderful dream home, this time with a bond. It was brick and timber architecturally designed beach house fully furnished with an upstairs inter-connecting walkway between two almost separate homes each with a bedroom, the most wonderful billiard table downstairs, and a self-contained kitchen. It was my dream home should Liane and I got hitched. Best of all, it was right opposite the beach, also on Peregian beachfront.

Shortly thereafter, Andrew Pizzey and I built both a huge braai and a jacuzzi. Andrew had me mixing cement. Boy was that tough.

David Allen came to stay for a few months and I gave him a patch of the garden which he had to tend for his keep. Later my best friend, Trevor Zabow visited from Sydney, then Hank Saacks and family. Jessica and Martine Allen also came back to stay.

Meanwhile I enjoyed playing at the local Coolum golf course where I coached the youngsters on a Saturday as the club never had a professional, and whose numbers rapidly increased to around 20 kids. We even had sleepover parties at my home watching golf videos.

We began expanding to places like Toowoomba, Gympie, Bundaberg, Dalby, Mackay, Airlie Beach, Townsville, and Cairns, as well as Brisbane and the Gold Coast, even Sydney. Our sign-written 'Rainbow Video' cars were everywhere. In all I opened 42 stores, and at the height of the operation, there were 68 franchise stores.

What made it so popular other than buying power? It was because the stores had substantial quantities of the latest new releases for the first few weeks before these copies were returned to the distributor. For instance, when Crocodile Dundee was released, we acquired 1,000 copies for just one store. Each store had literally thousands of videos which were written off over two years and then also sold for a profit on the second-hand market. The outside neon light branding was superb, as were the regional television adverts.

It seemed we were unstoppable, but there were more twists and turns.

My sister and Peter divorced around 1986. I now looked to open a video store on the exciting Gold Coast where there were young people, and a shul nearby. I found a great store in the middle of Broadbeach. But along came Peter, and he said he would sort out the lease, and would I go to Coolangatta and get his new store ready to open.

Of course, trusting Peter, I did just that. Then Peter informed me that he had signed the lease in his name, and was passing the store on to his brother George who had sold his Noosa store, and gave me $10 000 as hush money to disappear as they didn't want the competition from me on the Gold Coast given my previous success.

Of course I was furious and upset. At this stage I should have moved on into something useful, probably in Sydney, given my law degree, but instead I went and opened a store in Toowoomba. Toowoomba was cold in winter, and had little or no young social life.

Once again I opened the store by offering anyone free movie per day for two weeks. The rationale was to get clients into the store so they could view the thousands of videos including the fact that we had many copies of the latest releases so everyone could get what they wished to watch. At the same time it generated substantial income as clients tended to rent two movies at a time creating the cashflow. In addition, it simply wiped out the opposition video stores for those two weeks, and then the onus was on me to retain these customers.

Part of the marketing strategies was that every 30 minutes we would announce a movie title and if the person brought it to the counter they could rent it for free, at the same time when getting a video everyone also got a scratch card. One-in-five was a winner and that got them an additional free movie.

For kids we had a children's playroom with movies for them, toys, blackboard, as well as an aquarium. I also engaged a display man to make large items seen on video posters such as a treasure chest or a dinosaur. At different times of the year we would have action or horror weeks with the staff dressed up and the store recreating the respective environment. The clients flocked to the store and we were on our way.

Toowoomba was three-hour drive from Peregian, so I had a small room and shower built upstairs such that I could spend the night. I would stay three-four nights a week. I had employed some great staff including Belinda Harris (my former girlfriend), and sisters Kathryn McGowan and 21-year old beauty Allanah McLennan.

Allanah, slim with golden hair, basically seduced me, such that we had a romantic affair getting together every week when I came up. However, she also had another boyfriend on the side when I was not around.

I did connect with a wonderful Rhodesian couple from Mazoe, near Harare, Gloria and John Prentice. Gloria worked for the local television station and made up my tv adverts including one memorable advert for *Raiders of the Lost Ark* with her whole family participating, and which went on to win a 1985 Golden Spool award Queensland television 10.4. TV award, and another TV award in 1986. I later ended up staying with them on their Mazoe farm, near Harare in Zimbabwe.

I was to also receive best video retailer award (Video Business magazine) 1986, and 1988 Video Pioneer award (Australian Video Awards).

Around this time I also opened another store at Warwick, about an hour away, where it really gets cold in winter, and where it has a significant Italian population such that the Italian national rugby team would come and train. It was rather quiet, but still profitable, again with some really good staff.

Sometime later I was to hear that Allanah had told the staff she was going to marry me. It was not that I didn't like her, but marriage hadn't occurred to me. I guess I got cold feet as I was still in love with Liane. Then one day I invited Allanah to come stay at my Peregian Beach home. But no sooner had I left to travel to Toowoomba, than she invited her other boyfriend to come stay.

Martine Allen who was staying at the house (together with Jessica), simply threw them both out of the house. She would have nothing of the kind and intended to protect me.

Liane and I would still go out, at times it seemed romantic, but her interest strayed to Michael Allen when he visited, and flirtatious Peter Bell, so clearly warning bells. Nevertheless I was besotted and there were times when I still thought things would work out.

As a result of commuting to Toowoomba, I missed the newspaper headlines stating that the road the video store was situated in was now to become a ring road. This meant there was only one way in and then you could not turn around and return the way you had come. This was a disaster, as now a new competitor, Video Ezy, came along and opened two mega stores at either end of the ringroad with me locked in the middle. Turnover went down by 60%, and given that I was not working in the store, I decided to sell for whatever I could get, selling to the new owner of the Rainbow Video Head Office, Sid Morris. The same head office I was supposed to have a shareholding in.

Of course by then Peter should have taken the chain public, but he was too much of a control freak, which was sad, leading to discontent amongst the franchisees who approached me to lead a break away under my leadership, but I refused. Far too loyal. However, that never stopped his secretary whispering rumours into his ears and I had to put up with a tirade from him.

Following Peter's divorce from my sister, my expected half share in the chain was clearly no longer going to materialise. I had no formal agreement but, after all, 'he was my brother-in-law', another interesting lesson.

Bell also tried his hand at music concert promoting, a huge happening outside Brisbane with Midnight Oil, Australian Crawl, AC/DC, Men at Work, and others, but the elements were against him. It drizzled, but not enough to collect on the rain insurance, and with fans staying away, he lost a packet.

Then Bell moved into night clubs in Mooloolaba, enjoying his DJ music passion, and the ladies of the night. The hotels at Alexandra Headlands (who also had night clubs) adjoining their rooms took up his challenge, operating these clubs at cost, and eventually a bankrupt Peter had to close down. He never recovered from this setback.

Morris seemed like a regular guy. He had been farming and decided to enter the video industry. He bought the Toowoomba store for his son, and assured me that all the staff would be retained. Well that never lasted long as his son fired all the staff, then got bored and left the business leaving his dad to carry the can.

Around this time I opened a huge 5000sm store at Mackay with a partner, Sandy McKenzie (formerly from Kenya), who owned the Fairietale Castle at Bli Bli, and we also acquired a video store in Townsville which the former owners operated, whilst I was asked to open a store for Peter Allen in beautiful Cairns. Both stores did a roaring trade. Not long thereafter I flipped the Townsville store. At the same time I came across a video store at Airlie Beach which I bought with Faye and Les Purcell (the surf guru). I thought I could substantially improve the turnover.

Meanwhile I had my former employee, Mark Summers from Maroochydore go and manage the Cairns store even though Peter

Allen worked in it. Peter did not wish to let on that he owned the store, and that his father had bought it for him with another investor. This was later to have repercussions when it was discovered that this manager was stealing, and I was blamed for not overseeing the store some 1200 kms away.

To my dismay, much like Toowoomba, Mackay now built a ring road. We were again in a desperate state as Video Ezy once again opened a mega store, and our turnover tumbled. Our landlord was reluctant to release us from our substantial monthly lease. After a number of months losses he finally cancelled the lease and we had to pay a forfeit of $120, 000.

A very painful lesson learnt. Have a back-up plan, otherwise don't be greedy and incur a lot of debt.

After all that had gone before me I was left working at Airlie Beach on the Barrier Reef, the heart of the Whitsundays in what turned out to be the best time of my life.

My mom joined me in an apartment. But she couldn't walk anywhere and had to stay inside the air conditioned apartment as it was very humid while I was at work. Given that she knew no one and was very lonely, she eventually decided to return to Johannesburg and go into the Sandringham Jewish Aged Home. This was going to be very difficult for her given she had spent most of her life in Cape Town, but her brother and sister lived in Johannesburg.

I now shared the apartment with Beverly Freeman and we had a fun time. I made wonderful friends, and soon bought a brilliant home at the top of a cliff overlooking 73 islands, and later below Abel Point marina when it was built. It was known as the 'fun house' with Maria Anderson, John Musster, and David Sutton sharing the house. Andrew Pizzey built a wonderful deck which also overlooked

Abel Point marina from my deck   *Airlie Beach sunset from my deck*

the swimming pool as we gazed out over the barrier reef with yachts sailing by.

So in under three years I had two homes. Welcome to Australia the land of milk and honey, or so I thought.

Life was easy and free. You want to make some money, crew on a yacht, and swimming in the resort pools at midnight with friends, whilst I traded video rentals for pasta dinners with the owner, Luigi. What an idyllic lifestyle, walking to work.

Night time was spent roaming the balmy evening, watching toad racing, and flirting with girls at the nearest pub, or having a joint with Bill Smith, the owner of the Whitsunday Times, who had sailed his yacht from Hout Bay, Cape Town, to Airlie Beach. The best of times was just sitting on the deck with palm trees swaying and shooting the bull until midnight, enjoying the drink and the company.

We would go sailing with my golf partner Jim Theroux who owned the 1974 America's Cup boat, Southern Cross, Alan Bond's first boat (Ben Lexen designed) which lost 4-1 to the Americans, and I crewed and sailed with him, racing Wednesday evenings, starting at the back of the pack and then sweeping past all the yachts as we neared the finish.

1974 Americas Cup 'Southern Cross' cruising the barrier reef

Southern Cross chartered to Contiki groups, which were made up of 75% girls, so life could not be better, and I was so proud to be given a 2/5 rating for cooking. That's where I met Wafaa Bouraslin, an exquisite young lady from Beirut, Lebanon. Of course, given that I am Jewish, it was to be kept secret from her family, and sadly she eventually returned to Beirut at the height of the Israeli invasion. She kept in touch for a while, but eventually happily married the fellow who molested her, such seemed to have been the culture.

Those were the days before exclusive Hayman Island resort was built, and Hamilton Island resort, with the runway abutting the sea, and a quaint golf course having recently opened. Airlie Beach was the gateway to these islands with yachts leaving for charter and day trips from Shute Harbour, and celebrities like Cliff Richard roaming the streets. Mind you, it only had one main street with a

3000 population, and daily young travellers doubling and swelling the population.

The video store was central to the folk at Airlie and I soon met and became friends with the community, with 3000 young tourists passing through daily. The problem with this was that if you met someone they were mainly in-transit.

We played golf three times a week together with Jim, Andrew McKay, and Mike Carmody. Slowly my game returned and I started to practice. Balmy time, and numerous folk visited and stayed over and we would spend the evening chatting on the deck late into the night.

Although the store was not making much money, it paid my way, while Morris was still paying off the Toowoomba store with monthly payments which I was using to pay my $200, 000 bond for both of my homes. When my payments were completed I would sell one of the homes and take the profit.

Roundabout this time, my girlfriend, Fiona Barker, and I, decided to go away for a two-week holiday to Cairns. Living in a small town, with the next town, Proserpine, with a population of 10,000 was enough to make one go batty, so every now and then, you needed to get out.

No sooner had we driven off than I heard that a dear friend had passed on from cancer. It was sudden and we considered returning but kept going. The adventure of the open road to Cairns nine hours away was wonderful as the road followed the Barrier Reef, Bowen, Townsville, Mission Beach, white-water rafting at Tully, and Cairns. The road itself was one-lane with a dirt road on either side, so you played chicken with the oncoming traffic to see who would move over first, and of course overtaking had its challenges.

Stopping overnight along the way at the beautiful seaside town of Mission Beach (the new Airlie Beach) we had a wonderful romantic fish dinner, then onto Cairns. Modern, clean, balmy and air-conditioned as humidity can really rock the senses.

While in Cairns we took a rickety steam-engine railway trip winding our way up the escarpment through the mountain as we climbed up to the small tourist village of Karanda, and the market, full of creative items and people. I decided to have my fortune read by a clairvoyant using tarot cards.

Karanda is very alternative, and you could get anything from organic vegetables, to having your fortune told. This seemed fun, and I decided to see what the fortune teller had in store for me. Even though I never believed in such people, I was brought up in a homelife which included spiritualism, so I was very curious.

Oh, my gawd, I have never forgotten her chilling message! She dealt some cards, and I had to pick some of them. My final card turned out to be the 'card of death'![31] which spelt radical change coming to my life including long distance travel. Besides a little jolt, I thought nothing further thereon. Oh how wrong I was. The wheel of destiny was turning, painfully!

Heart fluttering there was nothing on my agenda which took in traveling, and I simply let her warning drift over my head as I went to watch musicians play and eat some of the delicacies.

With tourists heading out to the Barrier Reef three hours away on large shuttle speedboats, we headed for the wonderful tourist resort town of Port Douglas, and the swaying palm trees, where

---

31 The Death card signals that one major phase in your life is ending, and a new one is going to start. You need to close one door, so the new one will open. The past needs to be placed behind you, so you can focus your energy on what is ahead of you.

every day is paradise.

From there it was onto Cooktown, and the Daintree Forest. The wonderful thing especially about Northern Queensland is that many Kiwi Māori folk have relocated there, and the further north you go the more Aboriginal folk you meet. Coming from Cape Town I felt right at home with the mixed population. It reminded me of my former home, although I was now a naturalised Australian, and really happy with my new life.

David Sutton, Barry Cohen, Maria & John Musster, John Seargent, Andrew Pizzey

Everything had been so easy, and I had made wonderful friends. Eventually we returned to Airlie Beach, going crewing on the yacht Southern Cross, and marvelling at my wonderful life.

Around this time, I was painting the outside of my home when a railway sleeper beam literally fell on top of my head. I saw stars and flashing lights. When I fully came to, I realised there was a fountain of blood squirting out from the top of my head. Wrapping my head in a towel I made my way to the local doctor who did a wonderful job patching up the wound, which was very sensitive for the next few days.

Of course where I went, Video Ezy followed, and they opened another store nearby. Little did I know that one of their head office directors was a former Muizenberg fellow who had dated my cousin, Colin Resnick. By this time I thought I could do more with my life and qualification than just serve over the counter. So I decided to sell the store, which I did to Christopher de Dobi.

Now I dedicated myself to golf at the age of 39 with the intention of finally turning professional. After nine months practice, and playing off a scratch handicap, I was playing great golf. Excited, it was now time for my first pro tournament which I thought I was good enough to win.

Man proposes and G-D disposes. So much for my plans. So, there I was enjoying a drink in the balmy evening out on the deck listening to the clink of the lanyards on the yacht beams below at Abel Point marina and dreaming of the morning. As I made my way down the stairs, I suddenly tripped, and fell head-over-heels into the swimming pool.

My first thought was oh no, I hope I'm okay. Clambering out of the pool, my wrist seemed sore. One of my housemates, who was also a nurse had a look at my wrist, and then it was off to hospital about 30 minutes away in Proserpine, the other airport to the Whitsundays. It must have been around 23:00 when the wrist was finally x-rayed. By then it had swelled into a giant golf ball.

The swollen wrist was such that after an xray nothing showed up, or so I thought, so it was back home, we shaved my arm, and placed an ice-pack on it every two hours, while trying to catch some sleep.

Morning, as I made my way down to the practice range. There was Ian Baker-Finch, Brett Ogle, and Terry Price warming up. Excited, I gritted my teeth, and told myself I could play through the pain.

Dropping a bag of practice balls, I swung the club around, and found I could make a swing without much pain. But oh, my golly, I now tried to hit shots. Five practice shots later having urged myself to play through the pain and watching these shots travel only 20 metres I gave up my dream.

Dave Sutton and Barry Cohen, my arm in a sling, on my deck

Life can be strange. When the swelling subsided, I returned to the hospital. After further examination it was discovered that I had broken my wrist. Nine months of practice down the drain, as it would take another six months to heal. End of my golf career before it had started!

The norms of fate weren't finished with me. Now with work drying up, my housemates and close friends told me that it was time to leave and get on with their lives in Sydney. I was once again on my own, no real friends, and certainly no family.

I vaguely became aware that Australia was in the grip of a property crash. I didn't really know what that meant, but it was not long before Morris informed Sandy and I that he had invested heavily in property, and that he was no longer able to continue with his contracted monthly payments, and which I was using to pay my monthly property bonds.

It took a while before the reality struck home and panic set in. Tracing agents reported that Morris's son had bought them a house, but that Morris appeared to have no assets. It was a huge amount he owed! Litigation got us nowhere, and only at the doors on the Supreme Court did he sign the acknowledgment of debt, but then it was to prove 15 years of fruitless chasing him, and we were to get nothing.

Sandy simply wrote it off to tax. I had now lost everything I had worked for the last 10 years, as I panicked when I couldn't get work.

At the same time, Christopher de Doby who had expanded the video operation adding music and books, offered me a 5-year repayment deal to re-acquire the video store. This was a real good offer, but by now I was totally traumatised. I couldn't admit to failure. I had to find my way. Having been at the top, people couldn't understand how I had lost my money.

Now isolated in the outback, friends few and far between, my life imploded. I had never failed in my life and I had no coping mechanism.

Living in a small town, I could not get work. Of course, with a law degree I still thought I warranted a decent job. The days dragged on, there was no one I could turn to for advice, Australia was in a recession, and instead of discussing this with the bank, I panicked and listed both my dream homes on the market.

Yes, I was looking for work, but I was then both too depressed and too proud to take the menial job, nor sign on for government financial assistance which I thought was below me and I was then a bludger. I sunk lower and lower as the country settled into a countrywide recession. I just wanted it all to end.

Days dragged on and I became more desperate, and depressed. I had travelled to Sydney looking for work, and was sleeping under a staircase at a friend's townhouse. What a come down from being in semi-retirement. I went for an interview to run Hoyts Cinema, and with my background in film and business, I really thought I stood a good chance. A boy from back home, with whom I travelled daily on the train to school, was now the joint owner, and interviewed me. But I was not who he was looking for. He said I would be too ambitious.

By this stage all I wanted to do was return to South Africa, see my mom in Johannesburg and go on to Cape Town to see old friends, some family, and figure out a way forward.

No sooner had I arrived in Johannesburg and staying with my wealthy cousin, Spank, than he offered to buy a 50% shareholding in my Noosa Peregian beach property. Mind you, I priced it at a real bargain, and I suddenly relaxed. I could still retain an interest in my homes, and the rest of the trip was enjoyable, as I recovered from my fright.

Man proposes, G-d disposes....

One thing you learn in law is to consign everything to writing. I never did this with my brother-in-law Peter insofar as the video head office, and I should have learnt my lesson.

Growing up we were a very close family, and this included Spank, his brother Michael, and my aunt and uncle, so trusting, I took my cousin at his word.

Returning to Airlie Beach to pack up, my cousin kept me waiting for the signed agreement, stretching from two weeks, a month, and eventually nearly three months before he informed me that he had changed his mind. There was no explanation. I was devastated. Family had been so important to me, and the bubble had burst.

We were only to talk, have coffee, and reconcile 32 years later!

Depression is a terrible thing, as mentally I sunk lower and lower. Then as often happens, I received offers on both houses. Now what to do?

With the property market in decline, I had already turned down offers based on our agreement, and eventually I simply grabbed at another lower offer.

Having come from a tight family where our parents helped each other, and close bonding with cousins, I saw this as a family betrayal. I was deliberately offering a bargain, and it would not have placed a dent in his finances. With no work, and having to pack up my dream home, a deeper spiral of depression set in.

It was time to grow up, and realise I was not owed a living, and that I must stop relying on others and paddle my own canoe. This was my making, irrespective of who was to blame. It was time to plot a way forward, and not look back.

Back on the Sunshine Coast I attempted to reconnect with Liane staying a few days with her, but it was not to be. She later informed me she was still getting over a fellow she was madly in love with who had dumped her. Packing up both of my homes was devastating.

They were my dream homes and everything was going up in a cloud of smoke. I had basically given up a wonderful law career and wasted eight years of my life.

One of the placement agencies had me complete an evaluation, which was really interesting and, inter alia, stated *"Your profile indicates that you are a determined, persistent individual who will bring an intensive and comprehensive approach to the analysis of a problem or the evaluation of the practicality of an idea. You are an objective, analytical person who is a dispassionate anchor of reality. You will be calm, steady and persevering. You are tenacious after starting a project and you will fight hard for your objectives. You are independent and questioning in approach and you possess thoroughness and good follow-through for the projects that interest you".*

But then it continued to list areas of concern including that *I may not work well within a corporate structure, and as a team,* and that *I can be stubborn and opinionated, and may require force to change my approach, such that I may resist participation as part of a team, and may resent being forced to do things against my will, and work without supervision on difficult important assignments that are challenging.*

The more I tried the worse I became. It was a downward spiral. I was carrying so much pain. Of course I should have seen a doctor for some anti-depressant medication, but I never associated myself with failure, nor that a doctor could assist, and I was embarrassed to admit I needed help. I determined to return to South Africa and figure out my next move.

CHAPTER 6

SCRATCH CARDS: Back in Cape Town

Cape Town was exciting. The Rivonia trialists including Nelson Mandela, Andrew Mlangeni and, Oliver Tambo had been released from Robben Island after 28 years of captivity, and there was an air of optimism running through everyday life. India, the country who originally drove the banning of South Africa from the Olympics, were the first to invite a previously banned South African cricket team led by Clive Rice, to their country.

I stayed with my aunt and uncle. I was severely depressed and I would stay indoors or go into the garden with a blanket and jersey in summer to stop the shaking. I had never been to a psychologist or psychiatrist, but eventually I went to see someone who got me talking about expectations which hadn't been met. Eventually the flood gate opened and the tears started. Something I hadn't done since I was ten.

It was like parking a car but the cars on either side prevented you opening the door. You had two choices, drive forward into the wall and smash the car, or reverse and go in another direction, which fortunately I did.

After bumping into old friends with whom I had played rugby and attended law lectures, Harry and Jane Trisos, they invited me to stay for a while on their impressive property, 'Mile High' in Constantia. I was about to return (with luggage packed and in the car) to Australia when they managed to persuade me to stay longer. Harry offered me the opportunity to complete my law articles in his law firm, Molenaar & Trisos, which I accepted and completed the balance of my required two years. But then Molenaar was struck off the role for touting and the firm folded. Anyway I had enough of Molenaar, a tall 'pig of a man'.

Around this time, Hazel Green, the fundraiser for the South African Red Cross, who lived across the road from my uncle made enquiries about my interest in launching lottery scratch cards for Red Cross. She had heard that I had some knowledge of scratch cards given my involvement with Rainbow Video scratch cards.

These were commercial scratch cards but were unknown in South Africa, however I was being asked to launch a lottery operation.

This seemed a brilliant way to recoup my lost 'fortune'. If I had understood the real difference between commercial and lottery scratch cards I wonder whether I would have agreed. I struck the deal with Red Cross.

When I started this fundraising for Red Cross I only intended to do it for six months, and when the time was right, return to Queensland.

I quickly brought Harry on board, followed by a Muizenberg boy, Jonathan Gordon, an accountant who although a few years younger had grown up two roads from me opposite the park where we would play touch rugby. This was a good mix, and they received their equal shareholding for free. We launched *Scratch-it.*

It took off, with lottery cubicles crowded with people clamouring for scratch cards.

My life seemed to have turned a full circle. Whether the circle closes here or moves in other directions was for the future, and maybe it is fortunate that the future cannot be seen.

I grew up knowing scenery, the arts, and doing something useful and charitable with my life. I touched on various of these 'wants' in my formative years, and probably did law for reasons associated with my desire to help, and please my dad following in the footsteps of my grandfather.

Somewhere along the way I had unconsciously seen my former brother-in-law as an easy way into the arts. But I learnt the hard way that there are dishonest people everywhere and real friends are far fewer than imagined. This all had quite a devastating effect on me as I had to come to terms with the changing of my own value structure.

By way of interest, Sid Morris, who did me in over the sale of my video interests and over whom I held judgement but was unable to claim, was charged for fraud over a cheque he gave someone in 1989. What goes around comes around.

It was at this time the guys persuaded me to bring on a fourth person, tall sporty Iain McNaughton who had some experience in scratch cards. As far as I could tell he was a confident bullshitter. I threatened to leave the operation if he came on board, but eventually relented.

Putting together a professional team of legal, educational, and accounting personnel instead of trying to do it myself appeared to be the way to go. We were being recognised as a very professional outfit, and whereas we entered the lottery welfare market last without financial backing we had planning and administrative skills which were now propelling us to the fore.

Initially I was the only one full-time, but my partners then followed once it appeared to succeed, and this allowed me to become very creative, something which they encouraged, such that I was seen as an 'arrowhead' or a 'mover and shaker'. As such, I found a real niche and learnt more about my own abilities to foresee future developments, plot, plan, and above all be creative. This together with the ability to communicate well, really increased my confidence.

I had never had this form of support before, nor had been able to deal in business at such a top level. I really enjoyed what I was doing, felt like I was making a huge difference in many people's lives, and I was revelling in the challenge. This success allowed me to travel, taking me to places such as once again to the Okavango Delta for the holiday of a lifetime.

Now here I am, once again in the middle of the delta, no radios, VCRs, TVs or newspapers. Just you and the elements. Water, rivers, reeds, grass, trees, and green everywhere. The sky is overcast with patches of blue, hot, humid, with birds singing, and the sound of bush all around.

The last night was classic, pouring rain, but warm, lashing the dining area as we ate a hearty meal of oxtail and trifle by candlelight polishing off bottles of red and white in absolutely the middle of nowhere.

The previous day I went down the waterways by 'mokoro' (a hand-whittled canoe used for punting in the delta, often made from the wood of an ebony or sausage tree) paddled by my guide. We went quite a way and then walked amongst the animals for about three to four hours armed only with an axe.

We saw all forms of birdlife, zebras, kudu, impala, letchwe, warthog, phew no lions, but we came across two kills. I thought that was pretty good. No ways ....

In the morning we left by mokoro at 06:30 and as we came to where we were swimming yesterday, two crocodiles slid into the water only ten metres from us. We pushed on. The mokoro rippling through the water makes a wonderful gurgling sound as we moved through the everglades, over lillypads with beautiful flowers spread out to the sky and fish darting all about us bubbling as they went by. Birds chirped and ducks swam, whilst the fish eagles looked on benignly thinking about a fish breakfast.

Soon we saw a sitatunga (small buck), very rare, shy, and hardly ever seen. My guide said I was a very lucky person. Lucky certainly, for as we rounded another bend two more crocs slid into the water, but this time they made for us.

Boy, I never knew a mokoro could go in reverse, but there we were, flying backwards. Obviously neither of us wanted to be breakfast. Finally we turned around and retreated, the crocs just disappearing without a sound. To think I swam and splashed carefree in these waters yesterday. I think I'll swim in the shower now.

Later we went looking for hippos. We walked and walked barefoot through the bush and the swamp ankle deep in water over reeds sighting herds of reedbuck, impala, and letchwe until finally we tracked down three huge hippos swimming in their watering hole. Not too close. These guys can motor if they sense you given their very poor eyesight. Get hit by one of them and you'll not be around to tell the tale.

Then lying in my tent listening to the rain, I could hear the monkeys in the trees and a hyaena scratching at the tent flap. I wonder what next? And the guy doing the 'Camel' ads thought he knew what it was all about ....

As mentioned we started with scratchcards in South Africa, spread to Botswana (formerly Bechuanaland) and Nambia (formerly South West Africa).

Somehow we managed to get it off the ground and set up sales outlets throughout South Africa which Jonathan and Iain controlled.

But it wasn't too long before there were arguments between the four of us pulling our weight. With three you can make decisions, but four could be alone an impasse.

Around this time we also decided to enter the commercial scratchcard industry, something that was still unknown in South Africa.

Iain and Jonathan unsuccessfully presented a proposal I devised to the Sunday Times. I couldn't believe they would reject it as it was excellent and simple, so I got on the next flight and re-presented myself. The proposal involved an inkjet number on the front page with winning number printed inside the newspaper.

This had never been done in the print media, and became an instant hit, with the Sunday Times recording their highest monthly sale increase ever.

With this success we expanded into ink-jet games for other newspapers and magazines.

Meanwhile, I also got the guys to place a scratch card at a premium rate on the telephone. This option had only just been introduced and it went crazy. In the first month we took over R1-million. It seemed that possibly the hired help were phoning in from their places of work. The recording would then scratch the card over the phone, and the home owner would end up paying the phone bill.

By this stage we were also working with two UK fellows. Given the success of the phone project we went to the V&A Waterfront to celebrate where we drank Dom Perignon champagne. We reckoned another six months and we would each make a million. But just as we had got to the top the premium rate (0055) industry was closed down.

By now I was living at Barley Bay (just past Camps Bay) in the downstairs area of a house opposite the sea. Although only ten minutes from Cape Town and work, it retained a village atmosphere and was rather isolated from the city and suburbs, such that I would often forget that I was in South Africa as I gazed out to sea and watched the golden sunsets from the porch.

What fun to sit on the lawn and watch the cyclists wizz past during the Two-Ocean Cycle race. Every morning early it was a run to Clifton, and maybe a swim at the little protected beach below where the water was warm, and various folk came to stay. I really felt I was slowly getting my life back. The intention was still to return to Australia but at least I would have funds behind me.

As mentioned, I had also opened an operation with Lady

Khama[32] in Botswana in aid of Red Cross. She was the wife if the first President, Sir Seretse Khama (and mother of the future President Ian Khama), who caused such an international stir being the President's 'white' English wife. They lived on a very normal farm on the outskirts of Gaborone, where we had tea, nothing suggesting he was the president. Meanwhile we had entered into a distribution agreement with a very prominent local businessman, John Mynhardt.

Lady Khama was quite austere, stern, but fair. Sales really rocketed and money was pouring in to Red Cross, and I ran this operation.

When Kentumile Masire took over as President after Sir Seretse passed away, Lady Masire oversaw the Red Cross operation. Lady Masire[33] reminded me of a kind aunt. I think we really liked each other, and it wasn't long before she had her daughter, Matsudiso (Tsidi) travel around the country making introductions and booking me into her father's luxury accommodation, so ostentatious.

Tsidi also taught me about manners. I wanted to engage with a pedestrian I was to get out of the car and address them, because doing it from the car window was rude. She liked me. I must admit I found it humorous that when the President saw me at Government House he rushed back inside to put on his jacket.

They invited me to a state dinner with dignitaries and ambassadors from across the continent dressed in traditional attire. It so happened my beautiful 18-year old niece, Mandi, was visiting and I took her to the banquet as my partner. We were seated with all the

---

32 **Lady Ruth Khama** was the wife of Botswana's first president Sir Seretse Khama, the Paramount Chief of its Bamangwato tribe. She served as the inaugural First Lady of Botswana from 1966 to 1980.

33 **Lady Gladys Masire** was a Botswana teacher and political figure who served as the longest ruling First Lady of Botswana from 1980 until 1998.

cabinet ministers and it was with great delight I saw them hand out their calling cards to her. What a way to arrive and be exposed to the 'African way'.

Then it was gliding across the dance floor with all the togos and amazing African traditional dress including Lady and President Masire.

We then branched out into both commercial games and more traditional forms such as scratchcard for Anglo American shopping centres in South Africa and other centres in the UK. At this time I also registered for a one-year fundraising diploma with UNISA.

Like usual, though, my plans were to change. At this stage I was still single and wondered whether I would be prepared to give up my bachelorhood, the peacefulness and non-responsibility, to actually marry and have children, a family. Yes, I love children, but then I had only had them in small doses and never had to live with them other than my nephew and niece.

An old girlfriend who I took out in Queensland, a children's television presenter-producer of *Totally Wild*, Angela Brown (mother from Thursday Island and father Scottish), and with whom I had fallen crazily in love the moment she opened her mouth to talk, was upset when I left Australia, and was supposed to join me in Africa, but for the second time she got cold feet.

Meanwhile I diverted my energies back into golf which I still enjoyed and played quite well, although not as well as on the Barrier Reef.

And what of South Africa and more particularly Cape Town? Cape Town, what a change. With the abolition of apartheid there were fleamarkets everywhere including St George's Mall in the city, but more than that, there's music. Buskers playing all sorts of instruments and music from jazz to pop to traditional African, with groups as far afield as Nigeria. Wherever you went, there was now music and laughter despite the recession.

This was particularly noticeable at the docks where the Waterfront had been redeveloped with many eating establishments, bars, pubs, shops and music all over. Even at 2am it was still buzzing with thousands of people. During December millions of tourists visited, with twelve cinemas, live venues and theatres. As you can imagine, the development keeps progressing.

The races in Cape Town mix very freely but there are still heaps of problems in Gauteng (Transvaal) and Kwa-Zulu Natal (Natal) as whites came to terms with the change of government and the cultural transitional change occurring as the country moved more towards socialism.

It was however pleasing to note that the ANC called for the dropping of all sanctions and African countries were falling over each other to form links with South Africa whom they now saw as their saviour.

Meanwhile South Africa re-entered the sporting arena, their limited abilities sobered the cockiness of the population, but they were quick learners and it wasn't be long before South African teams and individuals became a major force.

As to friends, besides my partners, I had very few. Most had emigrated and maybe I was working too hard, or I just didn't make the effort. My thoughts often strayed to friends in Australia.

Back to the Okavango Delta on one of my trips. Driving from Francistown to Maun to catch a 15:00 flight into the Delta, it looked as if I would arrive at 13:30. Hell, nothing to worry about, I'm in a brand new Avis rental car. Well think again buddy boy!

Three hundred kilometres from Maun in the middle of nowhere, no houses or petrol station, and bang the radiator is punctured, we go into overheat.

Okay, nothing to worry about, plenty of time, let the car cool down and I'll get some water in Coke cans from the river. Finally we're off again, plenty of time. 10 kms later, no water and we're overheating again.

Cruising along at 10 km per hour, I see a Motswanan who informs me there's a game conservation African village 1 km into the bush. They help with water and mielie meal which we washed down into the radiator thereby plugging the hole. Off again, flying at 160 km per hour, going to arrive at 14:45 in the nick of time. Wrong again, 50 km from Maun the mielie meal gives out, overheat and engine packs up.

I hitched a ride on the back of a bakkie with a family of Motswanas and missed my plane.

Now we were asked by the International Red Cross to see if we could expand our Red Cross scratch card fundraising project further into Africa.

Winging my way to Zimbabwe and Lilongwe, (Malawi) as the dazzling purple sunset glows and beckons, I wonder ... what next?

Of more interest at present is South Africa. Here we had absorbed one of our competitors and had been asked to consider taking over the management of our major competition VIVA.

This all goes well for the possibility of launching the National Lottery. Naturally we were excited as we thought we were really in with a chance. Even more so as another major group, Millionex, backed by the 9th wealthiest family in South Africa want to join us and their backers, Abe and Solly Krok, we hear, will put up the money for the lottery.

This will come as an interesting development to VIVA (backed by Liberty Life) who had already approached us (and Community Chest) to launch such a lottery. Together we now are the administrative centre controlling distribution with financial muscle. The next 6 months could be interesting.

But a month later we received a letter from the government informing us of the impending national lottery. This meant closing down ours.

In addition, our team dynamic was not gelling, and with a national lottery imminent, Harry left to start his own IT operation. Suddenly I found Jonathan, whom I had grown up with around the corner, siding with Iain and I was being sidelined. At this juncture I had made progress concerning the setting up of a regional SADC lottery which would exclude South Africa.

There was a lottery convention in the USA, and Jonathan and Iain wanted to attend while I ran the operation at home. I thought nothing of it, and when they returned they seemed to be bursting with energy. Iain indicated he wanted to be more involved with the SADC lottery.

One Saturday morning three months later I needed to go into work to retrieve a document. When I couldn't find it in my office, I went into Iain's office and opened his drawer, the first time I'd entered his office without him.

Low and behold, there was a contract for $10 million with a major US Gaming company to back the SADC lottery signed at the US lottery convention, but that wasn't all. In the document it stated that Iain and Jonathan had both founded the company and were the sole shareholders. I was gobsmacked!

Chapter 6

While I was digesting this, Jonathan came into the office and I hid under Iain's desk. In hindsight I should probably have confronted him, but of course there would be the question as to why I was rummaging through Iain's desk.

My next step was to approach a major law firm, where I was told I would need a war chest. Once Iain and Jonathan's duplicity came out I should take all precautions, and keep my curtains drawn. People have been terminated for less.

I issued summons and then confronted the boys, who refused to apologise. Jonathan informed me that they intended to inform and include me. What rubbish! I founded the company, reduced my shareholding and gave them shares for free, and put together this pending SADC lottery.

I wonder what my reaction would've been if they had admitted the deception. After all, after three months they must've been so close to launching the project. Clearly the game was up. Maybe they thought they could still salvage the operation on their own. But the more they denied, the more they put my back up. We could've worked something out, even if I didn't like what they had done.

I dropped the legal procedure due to the potential cost, but in anger I wrote to the USA lottery company informing them as to the true nature of the situation.

In hindsight, this was possibly a mistake given my financial situation. Maybe I should have taken my cut, and walked away.

They basically offered for me to continue with the commercial magazine and newspaper scratch cards, but I was so hurt I simply walked out. I couldn't work with either of them again, especially McNaughton.

I like to think that Jonathan was influenced by the tall older fellow. Once again my trusting nature had been taken advantage of. Another BETRAYAL!

Now what?

A week later I was down to play in the SA Amateur Golf Championships at Royal Cape. I had managed to get back to a scratch handicap, although I was not in the same form or head space I had been at Airlie Beach (with a 3-handicap or less you could turn professional). The betrayal, especially by Jonathan had taken its toll.

Teeing off I found myself playing against some future iconic names like Rory Sabbatini[34], Tim Clark[35], and Darren Fichardt[36]. It didn't take me long to understand that I simply didn't hit the ball far enough. While playing the 18th I hit a 5-iron for my second whereas they were hitting 8 and 9-irons. They also easily reached the par 5s in two. My friend, David Frost had already told me I needed to increase my swing speed, although I thought I was swinging flat out. I took a decision there and then never to compete again in a major open, and simply play golf for fun.

It was a promise I basically kept although I twice represented South Africa at La Manga, Spain, in the World Corporate Golf Championship (WCGC) where around 24 countries competed and in which I won the one-time returning home to my family with a case full of glassware. It was a proud nervous moment when they

---

34 **Rory Sabbatini** won six times on the PGA Tour and was runner-up in the 2007 Masters. He spent 21 weeks in the world top-10 in late-2007 and early-2008, with a high of 8th. Sabbatini won the silver medal at the 2020 Summer Olympics.

35 **Timothy Clark** formerly played on the PGA Tour. His biggest win was The Players Championship in 2010, which was also his first PGA Tour win.

36 **Darren Fichardt** won the Southern Africa Tour Order of Merit in 1999/2000 and 2003/04, won 7 European Tour events and 19 victory on the Sunshine Tour including the SA Open.

Our team at the World Corporate Golf Championship

announced*: "On the first tee from South Africa, Barry Cohen".*

Interestingly our South African team also included the ambassador to Spain, Bruce Koalane, later to be the fall guy in the Gupta

Waterkloof airport wedding landing scandal, who was then rewarded with another ambassadorial appointment to the Netherlands. He was actually a very good golfer playing at least four times a week 'as was expected from an ambassador'.

I also organised the world finals of the WCGC at George played at the Fancourt and Oubaai courses. A huge success.

Lesson learned

It is true there was no way I could have known about my colleagues lottery contract abroad, but that does not mean you should implicitly trust your partners. They are just like anyone else and can succumb to such a huge financial temptation. The fact that Jonathan grew up in the same small seaside town and that he was Jewish is no excuse for making exceptions. Everyone is to be treated equally.

However, the real lesson is not to lose your composure. In this case, there was little I could do. Agreements had been signed. I could have found a solution with my partners such that I could have been included in the deal or they could have bought me out. I needed the money. Instead I succumbed to my anger and shot myself in the foot simply to prevent them benefiting.

Anger is not the solution. Try thinking ahead as to what is in your best interest.

CHAPTER 7

SUPERSPORT Dream League & Dream Team

What do I now do?

That is always the question. I'm supposed to be the ideas man, the 'arrow-head', and so it came to pass that I noticed Fantasy Football had commenced in England particularly the Daily Telegraph.

The son of a Natal sugar magnate had started it and I journeyed to London to meet with him and acquire the rights to operate it in South Africa.

Around this time, given that I was in the gaming arena, I was asked by the UK Weekly Telegraph to run their Fantasy Football worldwide. What this entailed was placing entry forms in their newspaper, collecting and collating the entries from around the world, then receiving the results from the UK, based on the Premier League football results, and how individual players, given their position scored points that week. Individual results were then entered into a table and entries were individually tabulated. Time was of the essence because newspaper buyers who played the game would want to see the latest results in the newspaper they'd just bought.

PC glitches were now becoming problematic especially concerning the Weekly Telegraph causing problems when deadlines could not be met despite our best efforts, and eventually I lost the contract.

But it didn't take long for me to realise that Fantasy League was totally unknown in South Africa. I devised Fantasy games for Rugby and Cricket. I met with Louis Luyt, the rugby supremo, who was very keen to proceed. Luyt was a divisive person, a junior springbok lock and one of the wealthiest men in the country, but before proceeding I also met with Ali Bacher, the head of the cricket body and former iconic captain of the SA cricket team, who after two minutes told me to proceed but that I must launch cricket before rugby.

Now I was involved with my other passion – sport!

Before long we were up and running as I concluded deals with the Independent Newspaper group to feature the entry forms and the weekly results given that it would increase their circulation. This was followed by sourcing substantial prizes from sponsors with the assistance of both Cricket SA and SARFU's sponsors.

Before long we were receiving maybe 30,000 entries, and after expanding this to golf majors, we had multiple games at one time. I must admit the staff worked really hard, especially when we had computer glitches as PCs were very new to us.

I now decided to take the concept to New Zealand, where I again linked with the newspapers and television, but this time I did something that has haunted me ever since. Travelling with a broken ankle in a moon boot, having tried to climb the first floor outside walls to my apartment after mislaying my key only to fall, I cut a deal with TVNZ, the national broadcaster.

I then journied to Auckland and Wellington where I tied up similar deals with the national rugby and cricket bodies, and the Independent newspaper group..

I had to return to New Zealand to conclude the TVNZ deal. They were excellent people to work with, but I had a brain fart. TVNZ were the national broadcaster and their were competitors There was Sky TV, the pay channel, much like SuperSport, but smaller.

I suddenly changed my mind, thinking I would be working with a similar group to SuperSport but I was sadly mistaken..

Sky TV were all business and cut throat. In hindsight, I regretted this decision, especially once I had given my word.

We called it Rugby Dream Team (Dream League was too close to Rugby League). It wasn't long before we launched and received 40,000 entries. I linked up with two fellows to run the operation whilst I would send them the results every Monday. We were flying, and I put together a Celebrity Team consisting of All Black iconic rugby players and commentators.

The ironic situation was given the rugby rivalry between the two nations here I was in Cape Town compiling the scores by watching each and every Super 12 rugby game and then sending the results to New Zealand where the local population thought it was a local effort.

All payments for me went across to Australia. I was hoping to save sufficient funds to purchase a property but first buy a property for my sister. I was a bit too optimistic, and whatever came through ended up with her.

Lesson learnt

This time I was to blame. I had given my word and sorted out a detailed contract although yet to sign. The deal was very fair, but I was greedy! Dishonest! Clearly I was not honourable as I had been taught. I had shook hands on the deal, and later I was disgusted with myself.

Greed is a very manipulative and addictive poison, much like smoking, drugs or alcohol. Once you are greedy and lose control of what is right, you are lost. After all, it is only money. I still carry that shame.

There was a lot of marketing especially the design of the adverts, entry forms and results, and these went into numerous publications and newspapers. In order to cope with this I worked with a team of four girls who were in their own relationships. They also had an engaging fellow assisting them, who they looked after, as he was unsuccessfully battling AIDS.

The one girl in particular took over the spending and placing of adverts. Without realising it I was running up a gigantic bill with this agency who had failed to forward me their invoices. I had taken my eye off the finance ball, leaving it to the advertising agency.

Of course this was my fault as stupidly I thought they were spending in line with my budget, which they did insofar as purchasing advertising space, but not for their work, which now amounted to around R1-million.

Meanwhile I had been approached by Russell McMillan of Mnet SuperSport concerning the acquisition of the operation as long as I would work for them in television for three years minimum. At the same time the agency demanded their R1 million. I informed them of the possible deal, which was dragging on. They were using Barry Pogrund as their accountant. Barry lived opposite my aunt and uncle in Newlands, and was my cousin Andrew's best friend.

Together we agreed upon a deal, but then at the last minute, the girls clearly did not want to wait longer for the SuperSport deal. They asked me what was happening and I indicated there was still no confirmation, although I was fairly certain it would proceed as their lawyers were in the process of drafting contracts. But the girls decided to renege on our agreed deal, and now also insisted I sell my apartment.

A week later in 1997, the SuperSport deal started. We called it the SuperSport Dream League. All my debts were paid but the agency had lost out due to their impatience. I had answered all their questions truthfully, and left them to make their decision. Clearly I never used them again.

Now I saw an opportunity to take this concept for cricket to India and the West Indies.

What I never understood was the Indian Cricket Board and how wealthy and powerful these men were. Also, the political haggling when selecting their national team.

I made the arrangement and then had to travel to India via two cities with the chaotic traffic and motorbikes everywhere before I could meet with them as they were in a board meeting. Our meeting only occurred walking from one meeting room to another. I never heard from them. A long way to travel.

The West Indies was different, as the marketing manager was someone I knew. He had previously worked at Shell across the road from my office.

The West Indian board housed me at the Hilton in Barbados for nine days together with board members and the West Indian team. What a privilege. As we travelled around to meetings with television and the media it was wonderful to see messages in shop windows wishing the Windies good luck in their upcoming test against Australian. Night-time there was music in the city, and everything was so colourful.

Then the test began. We travelled from the hotel to the ground collecting the WI iconic music legends who were to perform at lunch, but it was a huge success with the watching crowd. A different freer society with much gaiety and less politics.

Now for the real treat, I sat in the Windies board box for the next five days with all the legends of my time. Sitting with me was Carl Hooper, Clive Lloyd, Michael Holding, Gordon Greenidge,

Gus Logie, Garfield Sobers, and 50-year-old legend Viv Richards who looked so healthy and fit that he could still go out and bat for the Windies. Now for the test.

By day three it looked like the game was over and would end, but then Brian Lara rose to the occasion with a century, and the Windies won by one-wicket. Unfortunately, the project never proceeded despite the goodwill.

Day 5: Lara stands tall to lead West Indies from front – Peter Deeley in Bridgetown

Brian Lara is famous for mammoth scores, but his century here must surely rank as the most momentous innings of his life with the West Indies captain attempting to steer his side towards one of history's more improbable Test victories.

Brian Lara celebrated with teammates after they won the third test against Australia by one wicket

It had all the ingredients of a high-class drama: a battle against the odds, shots of breathtaking quality, his name ringing from the crowded stands – and to boot, a full-blooded row with Australian fast bowler Glenn McGrath when both players had to be separated by colleagues.

McGrath put Australia in the driving seat with two lbw decisions in successive balls to reduce West Indies to 248 for eight as Lara looked on in anguish. It also meant that with only tail-enders Curtly Ambrose and Courtney Walsh to help him, Lara had to get the remaining 60 runs virtually on his own.

The loss of two West Indies wickets well within the first hour for the addition of only 20 runs was a poor omen for the home crowd, who had packed Kensington Oval on this working day hoping to see a win against all the odds. Gillespie eventually got back into the action and immediately troubled Lara but at the other end trouble of a different sort erupted. McGrath bowled a short ball which Lara went to duck, but it came through low and hit him on the helmet. Feeling his head, Lara was called for a leg-bye and when he arrived at the other end had a bitter altercation with McGrath. Whatever was said further angered both men and Adams had to come up and pull Lara away while Michael Slater intervened on the bowler's behalf.

The two protagonists continued their bickering for some time. When McGrath tried another bouncer Lara contemptuously pulled it for four.

*The West Indies captain was continuously urging himself on, talking and banging his side with his fist. Warne came back and Lara waited only two balls before he bounced down the pitch and delivered the leg-spinner high back over his head for his 14th fo*ur and his hundred, which had taken just under four hours.

I reported the idea of performers entertaining the spectators during lunch. After all, these cricket test matches were about entertainment, but Ali simply laughed it off. I guess he was too old fashioned and set in his ways.

The next few years was a brilliant time as I worked with the SuperSport inner circle of Heinrich Enslin (CEO), Glen Marques (future CEO), Andre de Villiers (MM) and Imtiaz Patel (future CEO). They provided amazing adverts and coverage on SuperSport with weekly slots in which I sometimes appeared.

Further games were expanded to F1 racing, GP Motorbikes, Golf majors, New Zealand Rugby and Cricket, Olympics, and English Football and also rugby in Australia, besides 100,000 Fantasy Football entries for the Weekly Telegraph.

I was sometimes operating eight games a week, with each having their own 5–7-minute slot on television, where I would sometimes appear as a guest on Hey, Hey, it's Saturday with Terry Paine who went out of his way to calm me.

Clearly deadlines were tight. I and Bob Pierce, who had also joined me, would have to watch every Super 12 rugby game recording the scoring manually as it occurred. But it was such fun being paid to watch sport!

We changed the name to SuperSport Dream League, and I travelled monthly to our head office in Johannesburg for board meetings. They were true to their word engaging with their advertising agency, flighting numerous brilliant Dream League adverts weekly. Whilst I published the SuperSport Dream League magazine (*John Dobson, who presently coaches the Stormers, and who appears to be the likely Springbok coach, produced the magazine*). Thousands of entries were received, and we were off and running. I was also well paid. Life was sweet.

Could anything go wrong?

One of our games had someone win both a motor car and a holiday trip, our 1st and 2nd prize. How could this be?

It was almost impossible to win once, let alone twice and he was interviewed on television. When he won again it was clear he was cheating, but how?

After an investigation I deduced that he would post in his weekly entries. It was stamped dated correctly by the Post Office, so how was he doing it?

It took a visit to his Post Office to understand what he was doing. The Post Office was on two levels. Downstairs to receive and upstairs to post. He would get the envelope stamped on the pretext that he was going upstairs to post the letter, then wait until the results came out the following day before making his selections. The crook! We told him he was cheating and there was no prize, and never heard from him again. He seemed such a nice fellow.

The days were not without romance as there was **Renee Ballin** whom I met 1996 at my friend, Tamara Saack's fiancé, Andre Gersohn's, bachelor party at the Waterfront.

Renee approached Andre whom she knew in a short middrift, to wish him on his engagement. There was a crowd of guys at the table, and no doubt she was fishing. She was very pretty, weighing only 56 kg and I immediately took the bait, as we walked and talked into the night along the pier.

Our relationship developed, but in truth there were glitches. Renee felt I was possibly too old for her with a 14 year gap.

CHAPTER 8
Touring with the SPRINGBOKS

It was around this time Renee and I got married on a grape farm in Constantia on the shortest day of the year, 21 June, and the sun was streaming down. We had recently visited Victoria Falls where we went white-water rafting. The Zambezi was up running at around 4,0 so it was going to be a fast run.

At the outset the boats were in calm water and we were instructed to jump into the water and get wet. Renee refused. Why should she, the water was calm.

No sooner had we reached the first rapids than Renee sitting at the front admiring the scenery received a mouthful of water direct into her face. Now wanting to get off the boat she was informed that was impossible also there were wild animals. Renee was happy to face them. From there onwards white knuckles gripping the boat, like a buck caught in the headlights, Renee held on for dear life.

For our honeymoon, we flew to Sydney where my friend Trevor Zabow had organised a get-together with all our old school friends, but before that we touched down to refuel at Perth.

Renee now refused to get off the plane. She felt I wasn't paying her enough attention. That was until she was ordered off. Shortly afterwards it was time to depart, but now she wouldn't get back on. That was it! The captain threatened that they were going to leave her behind with her luggage. Renee cooperated.

After Sydney it was onto the Barrier Reef landing at Hamilton Island and straight onto the 1973 Americas Cup yacht *Southern Cross* which my friend Jim Theroux had waiting for us. I thought we would relocate to Australia but Renee couldn't leave her family, and it was not to be.

Soon we had a most beautiful family as Jenna, followed by Rory, entered the world.

My regular interactions with SA Rugby Football Union (SARFU) had brought me into contact with Rian Oberholzer (CEO) and Gary Grant (marketing manager), who had got me to join them for a regular game of golf, mostly at Strand Golf course (where Rian was a member of Parow Golf Club). I suggested to them that I launch the Springbok Supporters Club worldwide.

The objective of the club was to gather a database of supporters to whom we could enhance the Springbok brand supply match tickets and merchandise, host dinners and golf days for the Springboks wherever they played a test match, both locally and abroad.

Wynand Claassen, an architect by trade, and captain on the troubled New Zealand tour in 1981 was the club's chairman, and we became good friends. He presented me with a Springbok blazer which I was very proud of, but hardly wore as I never 'earned it'. (*I *later donated it to the Springbok Rugby Museum.*)

SARFU were supportive and managed to get ABSA to sponsor the project, with ABSA launching their own Springbok rugby Visa credit card. ABSA started advertising their involvement such that soon there was an uptake of 40,000 credit card holders and 37 supporters' clubs from as far afield as England, New Zealand, the USA, and Afghanistan.

I was also publishing my own glossy Springbok Supporter Club magazines again with the assistance of John Dobson, whilst we were producing our own supporter club merchandise. My plan was to set up a franchise operations of different tier supporter clubs drawing on my Rainbow Video franchise experience, namely I offered franchises for countries where the Springboks played rugby tests and those where they did not, and offer benefits accordingly.

For rugby test playing countries there was a franchise fee, and in return they would assist me with the golf and dinners where they received a substantial cut, whereas non-playing countries did not pay a fee for the first two years while they built up their membership.

This would mean supporter magazines, braais, and get-togethers. We could allocate them test tickets and have the Springboks attend their supporter dinners prior to the test matches where they would sign autographs and the fans. Further, they could purchase supporter clothing. Meanwhile we set about assisting ABSA to sign up Springbok VISA credit card members.

Before I proceeded I obtained SuperSport's permission to do both projects. I was confident we were making a success. Fanatical supporters communicated with me sending me presents like Springbok blankets. Our offices in the city were now draped with the springbok colours. Meanwhile Dream League and Dream Team continued.

Eventually SuperSport decided to sell Dream League internally to their sister IT body 'Mweb', with the intention of making it into the main gaming portal in Africa. I was both very excited but also wary .

Well, you guessed it, nothing stays static. Three months later, the dot-com implosion happened, last in, first out, and out we went. Dream League closed, although today it is seen in another format, an improved computer driven format such as Superbru and Fantasy League.

Meanwhile, I was meeting and interacting with many like-minded rugby folk, including Jake White[37] with whom I had become friends (he was a Junior Springbok golfer), who enquired if I could employ his wife Debbie. Of course I was also meeting with many present and past Springboks, and now I was traveling with the Springboks and hosting braais with supporters at each venue prior to in-bound test matches.

In Port Elizabeth I received a surprise approach from André Markgraaff[38], who had been the Springbok coach prior to him being exposed in a racist revenge sting. Clearly an excellent former

---

37 **Jake White** is a rugby union coach and former coach of the Springboks – whom he coached to victory in 2007 Rugby World Cup and the 2004 Tri Nations. In 2011 he was inducted into the World Rugby Hall of Fame.

38 **André Markgraaff** a springbok lock and captain of the South African Barbarians on a tour to Europe and the Junior Springboks. He was a controversial national coach who resigned after he was revenged taped by Bester using the racial K-word after he was not selected for the Springboks.

springbok rugby player, he came up to thank me for what I had been doing for Springbok rugby. I was really touched that I had been noticed. Sometimes all we want is to be thanked.

It was around this time that I was giving serious thought to becoming an agent for professional rugby and golf players. South Africa was entering the professional era, I had my law degree and Springbok CJ van der Linde had asked me if we could join up in business, but it was not to be. I simply didn't have the confidence and we missed the boat.

I also had to give a speech at these events, and I was very nervous, quite scared to say anything, but at the same time I notice I enjoyed being out there talking to everyone, and I could make them laugh. Not all the speeches were fun, like the time I was on Afrikaans radio for an hour not only trying to understand the questions from the in-studio presenter, but questions from radio listeners and then having to reply in Afrikaans. I swore never again!

Another incident was when I was invited to attend the Springbok Awards dinner. SARFU were very good in inviting me to various events and I found myself sitting at a legendary table with five former Springbok captains and my heroes growing up. There was Abe and Avril Malan, Johann Claassens, Nelie Smith, Johan Marais, as well as Piet Uys. Not once did they bother to talk to me. Was it because they spoke Afrikaans and I English, or because they were part of a unique Springbok club and friends, while I was an interlooper. Either way, Piet told us an interesting story.

They were playing trials at Newlands for the Springbok team to tour New Zealand. The selectors were on the Grand Stand. A lineout opposite the Railway stand. Dirkie de Vos was throwing in the ball when Frik du Preez[39] said to him, *"No, not to me"*. Shortly thereafter there was another lineout this time in front of the Grandstand and the selectors. This time Frik said *"To me"*, and he rose imperiously as he took the ball, coming down he cradled it in his tummy, and turning to Dirkie: *"Now we both go to New Zealand"*. Well Frik went, but Dirkie was not selected.

Then came the exciting time to tour abroad with the Springboks to destinations such as Perth, Sydney and Brisbane, Wellington and Auckland, London, and San Diego. I was the oldest support staff with the exception of Butch Watson-Smith (*who as a schoolboy I would watch playing for False Bay together with John Benn, Basil Bey, Louis de Waal, and Des Christian*), although I felt like a complete rookie.

Later Nick Mallet (Springbok coach) was the coach of the team which won the Grand Challenge with a team which included Fabien Galthie (present French coach) and legendary French flank Lauren Cabanne.

Rian then asked me to address the audience attending the 2000 International Rugby Convention in Cape Town and discuss the supporter club. As luck would have it, Francois Pienaar, the 1995 World Cup winning captain, and dynamic speaker, addressed the attendees immediately before me. What an act to follow! I thought I would be nervous, being shy and not used to speaking in public, but I really enjoyed it and found a new gear to my armour.

Our weekly Saturday morning golf games were fun as I got the inside story of what was going down with Springbok rugby, whilst my golf was very competitive and I would bet my life on sinking

---

39   **'Frik' du Preez** played in the flank or lock, and was an excellent all-round footballer, could kick and even drop kick, was a tower of strength in the line-out, and had a fantastic turn of speed and fine running skills with ball in hand. He was named the South Africa's rugby player of the 20th century.

any putt. Then it was off to Newlands to watch the rugby from the SARFU box. It seemed like I was doing a good job.

We hosted Springbok events in Durban, Johannesburg, Port Elizabeth and Cape Town, where the rugby board presented previously disadvantaged players with their Springbok blazers. I got them all to sign three Springbok shirts. This was the only autographed memorabilia these players signed, and I later donated it to the Chris Burger Fund to raise funds for injured rugby players.

This was also where I met Makaya Jack (1987 SARU Player of the year award), and where I was assured he would have played eighthman for the Springboks, probably captained them but for apartheid. He certainly looked the part.

At this Newlands reception before the Springboks were due to play, Stephen Fry, the 1955 Springbok captain introduced himself (and later took the time to write me a letter thanking me for what I was achieving). I was quite flattered, but saddened to meet up with one of my heroes, Doug Hopwood, who had lost a leg and was in a wheelchair. Somehow our heroes never age in our minds eye.

On the 2000 Tour to England we hosted a magnificent supporter dinner with the Springboks at The Royal Dorchester in the heart of London. Syd Nomis (our Jewish hero) the former Springbok wing was a lot of fun, Raymond Ackerman pitched with his right hand. Bobby Skinstad was the captain, and Nick Mallett[40] the coach of the Springbok team.

Nick and I had played a little golf together, and he told me that

---

40 **Nick Mallett** in 1979 Mallett attended the University of Oxford, where he won Blues in rugby union and cricket, famously hitting three sixes in one over off Ian Botham, and played two games for the Springboks in 1984 against the South American Jaguars. played for the Springboks in 1984. He also successfully coached the Springboks between 1997 and 2000 and was the head coach of Italy's rugby union team between 2007 and 2011.

one of the hardest things he ever had to do was fire Jake White.

Alan Solomons, an attorney, who had been his coach when he played for the University of Cape Town prior to being selected for the Springboks, gave him an ultimatum to get rid of his other assistant coach, Jake White, given that he was receiving too much media attention, calling him merely a *'video technician'*, or he would resign, such that, Nick now had to choose between two friends. Jake went on to win the 2007 World Cup as the Springbok coach.

Springbok coach (1997–2000), between August 1997 and December 1998, under Mallett's guidance, the Springboks went on a record winning streak of 17 consecutive test wins. As part of the unbeaten run the Springboks won the Tri Nations Series undefeated and beat several teams by record margins, including a 52–10 against France in Paris, a 68–10 win over Scotland in Edinburgh, a 33–0 defeat of Ireland and a 96–13 against Wales. The run ended when the Springbok team was defeated by England at Twickenham at the end of a long tour on 5 December 1998.

The relationship between Mallett and Gary Teichmann, one of South Africa's most successful team captains ever (with 36 wins), began to sour and Teichman was controversially excluded from the 1999 Rugby World Cup squad. Mallett looked for a new captain, first turning to Corné Krige then Rassie Erasmus, Joost van der Westhuizen and André Vos for a solution. In the end, despite the internal instability in the squad, the Springboks managed four consecutive wins and were finally knocked out of the championship in the semi-final by eventual winners Australia.

His mistake he said was probably dropping Gary Teichmann in favour of Skinstad for captain prior to leading up to the World Cup. Skinstad's inclusion in the 1999 World Cup squad at the expense of successful captain Teichmann was derisive in South Africa, and although South Africa finished third in the competition there were many who believed that had Teichmann been retained as captain for that tournament they would have won, even more so as Skinstad carried a leg injury into the competition, and made little impression.

In 2000, Mallett accused the South Africa Rugby Football Union (SARFU) of "greed" for selling Tri-Nations championship tickets at inflated prices. He had alienated the SARFU executive, and on 27 September he resigned as national coach at the start of a disciplinary hearing began into allegations that his comments had brought the game into disrepute. Some fans, upset by how he had treated Teichman and his team's sudden poor performance, were also keen to see him go.

In spite of his team's relatively poor performance and the internal strife that marred his final years as coach, Mallett remains one of South Africa's most successful coaches ever, having won 27 of the 38 tests played under his guidance and rewriting the record books several times.

After London, we hosted the Springboks in Houston, USA. Prior to our dinner, there was a dinner for the legendary Springbok flyhalf and Bulls icon, Naas Botha[41] by his former club, the Dallas Cowboys. Naas and I became acquainted after this, and later had some meals discussing the impending launch of the Golf Hall of Fame. He is quite a nice fellow and misunderstood by many.

In Houston it was great catching up at the game and dinner with our cyberclub and old friends Dr Steve Orlin, Marty Gluck, Stephen Kaplan, Wilf Krasin and some of their wives.

Some of those I played with on these golf days included legendary springbok captain and number eight Morne du Plessis

---

41 **'Naas' Botha** is a former rugby fly-half, who played for Northern Transvaal and the Springboks. He was voted Rugby Player of the Year in 1979, 1981, 1985 and 1987.

and Mallett, who was equally competitive and took charge. He played off an eight handicap and hit the ball a long way. Normally as the lowest handicapper I take charge, but there was no doubt who was in charge as Nick continually urged me to concentrate, and yes, we won the event and a few bottles of wine. I liked Nick.

Harry Viljoen, the new Springbok coach was going through a torrid time with his 'running only' policy and 'no kicking', even from within your own twenty-five.

Touring with him it was soon clear that the Afrikaans speaking players sat separately from the English contingent, and although Skinstad was the overall captain, Joost van der Westhuizen[42] held sway with the Afrikaners. Can't say I connected with Bobby, other than a few photos together. Maybe it was the age thing.

When Viljoen took over from Nick Mallett in the run-up to that tour he had promised South African rugby fans a new vision of a running team who win matches by scoring tries.

Not for his team the traditional virtues of South African rugby: a big pack, a flyhalf with a strong boot and suffocating defence. No, they were going to imitate the Aussies and win by running the opposition off their feet. It was a great idea, one which most South African rugby fans were enthusiastic about. Where Mallett relied on stifling defence and the boot of Van Straaten, Viljoen would come in with fresh ideas and the Boks would start scoring tries.

The only problem was that just as soon as Viljoen articulated his vision, he started to move away from it.

---

42 **Joost van der Westhuizen** was a Springbok rugby player who made 89 appearances in test matches, scoring 38 tries. He mostly played as a scrum-half and participated in three Rugby World Cups, most notably in the 1995 tournament, which was won by South Africa. He is widely regarded as one of the greatest scrum-halves of all time

It all started well enough. His first Test in charge was against Argentina in Buenos Aires. The Boks took the field with Montgomery at flyhalf, and goalkicker, and with instructions that they are not allowed to kick the ball – period. Viljoen wanted to show their players that if they trust their skills, they can score tries from anywhere on the field. It worked, sort of... at times the Boks were breathtaking and at other times they were woeful, but at least there was a plan.

They managed to force a 37-33 win, but people could see what he was trying to achieve.

The tour moved onto Ireland and Wales after that and although the game plan was not as strict as it was in Argentina, things were slowly improving.

Instead of sticking with Percy Montgomery at flyhalf as he had done throughout that tour, Viljoen opted for the conservative boot of Braam van Straaten because he needed a win against the English at Twickenham at the end of the tour and returned Montgomery to fullback to ease the pressure at home.

The Springboks still lost, but far more importantly, Viljoen had for the first and not the last time bowed to the pressures of the job. That was the first hint of things to come.

A year later when he again took a team to Twickenham his rugby philosophy had taken a 180-degree turn. Instead of the free-spirited running of the ball and trying to score tries from anywhere on the park, Viljoen relied on a heavy pack, a back division of big bruisers and a kicking flyhalf in Louis Koen.

The funny thing was that he still spoke about his process... that same process he spoke about when his side went nearly 70 minutes with his outside backs hardly ever seeing the ball.

However, things started to go really wrong when they lost the first test of 2001 against a team of French rookies at Ellis Park.

Criticism was muted again after wins against the French in Durban and over a patched-up Italy side in Port Elizabeth, but it was clear that there was little improvement.

The start of the Tri-Nations against the All Blacks at Newlands the Bok forwards put on a stunning display, totally dominating their opposition, but poor goalkicking and a match the Springboks should have won, was lost 12-3.

A week later against the Wallabies in Pretoria the side won 20-15 over the world champs. The forwards were great again.

A draw against the Aussies in Perth further raised the spirits of South African fans, but that was as good as it got in 2001. A thumping against the All Blacks in Auckland was a precursor of things to come.

Losses to France and England and an inept performance against the US Eagles would have been bad enough, but it is the way the side played, which was the biggest disappointment. Where barely 12 months before he had promised exciting, flowing rugby, now we were back in the 1970s. Anybody who saw the squad selection knew that plan A was to kick the ball and crash it up the middle, and that plan A was the only plan.

One morning at breakfast in Perth, coach Viljoen approached me, taking me by surprise, and asked whether I thought he should resign given that he was under huge media pressure from South Africa after some poor results.

Gosh, what does one say in such circumstances. I said that if he thought he could still win the World Cup then stay, otherwise resign. Shortly thereafter he resigned as Springbok coach in 2001 with five wins from eleven test matches, but I don't think my comments had any bearing.

Instead of taking a newer, smarter version of South African rugby to the next World Cup, his side had lost nearly as many games as they had won. And even worse, you never felt as if they were about to improve.

As much as Viljoen seemed to favour the upcountry players, Nick favoured the coastal players, particularly Skinstad, maybe because Nick played Number eight in his only two Test matches in 1984 although he should have played many more if he hadn't been the brash *'Engelsman'.*

I must admit touring back in Australia I felt I was returning home. Everything was familiar, and the supporters flocked to our gathering. Seeing tall Mark Andrews, the iconic gentle giant lock cuddling little babies, then prop Ollie le Roux from the Free State surprised me by informing me that his mom was Jewish and that his sister lived on a kibbutz in Israel.

Nick didn't like being told what to do by the rugby authorities running foul of them, and I organised a golf game between Rian Oberholzer and Nick at Parow Golf Club to try and resolve certain issues. There we were walking down the fairway two large fellows well over six foot and a small short guy in between, me. Must have looked funny, but at least I had played off scratch. It resolved nothing. Both liked being in charge and they just didn't like each other.

Gary Grant, Oberholzer's sidekick informed me that it had been agreed that the supporters' club would be given over to me as all parties seemed satisfied with the progress. It was at a family get together at my relative, Hal Shaper, the famous lyricist, that Selwyn Lewis from the Treble group (and Foschini family), sidled up to me and started quizzing me about the supporter club.

On one of the Springbok buses going to play England early December 2002, I noticed Gary and Rian were neither sitting with me nor including me in any conversation. This was even more blatantly clear on the return trip to the hotel. The air was frosty.

Not long afterwards I was given three months' notice and informed that the Foschini family guy, Lewis, had acquired a half share in the club and would be taking over the management. Oberholzer and I never spoke again.

I wondered what deal had been made, and with whom. The wheels of fortune were turning once again. The only consolation was that I received many kind messages of support from supporters.

What next.

CHAPTER 9

CANSA and the politics of transformation

By this stage I was now 50, married with a two-year old boy and a four-year-old girl, and no job.

Who would want to employ me?

It was time to change direction. I had always wanted to do something for welfare and the opportunity arose when I was fortunate to be selected to lead the Cancer Association of South Africa (CANSA) with nine regional offices, 390 employees, with an annual budget of R90 million, although it was losing R10 million annually. Unfortunately, our head office was in Johannesburg

It was clear to me that this was a centralised old fashion Afrikaans dominated organisation and I set about decentralising it, taking the palliative care services to the outback by training their own community members to look after those with cancer rather than send them to the city.

We started off by changing the logo to the present more modern one and introduced fundraising events like *Movember* (shaving hair and moustaches), licensing the CANSA "Seal of Recognition" brand logo, and expanding the Sanlam Cancer fundraising golf events raising substantial amounts. At the same time, I was meeting oncologists, anti-smoking campaigners, and sponsors.

I also visited our regional offices and had wonderful loyal support from my PA, Lorna Johnson. In Cape Town I worked with the Western Cape head of that division Niamaat Gamildien, whilst in Kwa-Zulu Natal I felt aggression from our African head. The reaction was *not another white guy* pulling the purse strings. What about transformation?

The board was also interesting, three whites and three people of colour, with the chairman, leading oncologist, Dr Georges de Mûelenaere, having the casting vote. Once again ignorance is bliss. I just went with the flow, but plots were brewing.

By this time, I was commuting three nights a week to Johannesburg. Was this problematic? I didn't think so. However, the board was questioning why I hadn't relocated to Johannesburg, which I knew was actually part of their job description, although I played dumb.

I had recently bought a wonderful double-storey in Hout Bay, perfect for my two young children, and I had just got my daughter into Llandudno Primary. Could we not continue to live here?

Attending a board meeting we were informed that there was a loophole in the constitution that allowed for a government appointee to the board, in this case Dr Precious Moloi, the wife of Patrice Motsepe, the wealthiest black man in South Africa and whose brother-in-law is now the president.

That meant that those board members of colour were now in the majority. Part of the reason for this takeover was the expectation that it would lead to additional funding from the government. From my point of view, I was happy to support and follow the direction of any board, but they never saw it that way...

We had a scheduled meeting of the board and regional heads. I arrived from the airport to find it was already in progress despite the fact that I was the CEO, with Gamildien chairing it. More alarming was that she made it clear to me that not only was I not in charge, but that the meeting had the support of board member Salome

Meyer, and that she was now in charge.

Moloi was not present due to her pregnancy and Kevin Wakeford[43] a former ANC operative had been invited to take her place. He was clearly the hatchet man.

He was very aggressive towards me and gave me three days to relocate to Johannesburg. It was clear this was a planned strategy. At the same time, he offered me an alternative option, head up the CANSA Trust, the organisation's funding arm. Given they were only paying me a gross salary of R30,000, way down on what I previously earned and not enough to cover my expenses, the thought of relocating and then being turfed out by the board as soon as they could find a reason, which is clearly what they were angling for, led me to accept the CANSA Trust position. After all it was also managing an annual budget of R90 million.

Gamildien who I had thought was an ally, was then elected as the new CEO. In fact, she told me that it was arranged. I was then to learn that she had spent time in Iran being trained and I wondered whether there was also an Anti-Semitic element.

Meyer and Gamildien were friends, and it was clear she had orchestrated this situation, which was strange as no one had ever raised an issue regarding my performance, quite the opposite.

I was furious, even more so when six weeks later the board informed me that they had made a decision to place the CANSA Trust back under the authority of Gamildien. They offered me a package to leave. Clearly this had been planned all along.

Meanwhile, Meyer in a disgusting power play triumphantly

---

43   **Kevin Wakeford** was the former CEO of the South African Chamber of Commerce before he was forced to resign. He was implicated in the Zondo commission Gupta scandal insofar as Bosasa and the matter was handed over to the police for investigation.

approached me: *"There are winners and losers, and you're the loser"*. Silently I replied, *"Not until the fat lady sings"*.

It was at this stage that I realised that NPOs were no different to the corporate world. It was dog eat dog as leaders abandoned a desire to help others and tried to manoeuvre to get power and access to the money.

The trade unions approached me enquiring whether I wanted their assistance, but I had no savings and couldn't afford to fight without an income. I had to take the package. Now I was back on the street.

It never ended here.

A year later both regional heads and the public approached me for assistance. It seemed Gamildien had made CANSA her personal fiefdom, increasing her salary from R240, 000 to close to R1-million per year, which was almost more than the President of South Africa was receiving at that time, employing her family members as well as board members on contract, including Meyer, contrary to CANSA's constitution, and going on overseas shopping trips with her family while supposedly attending cancer international conferences in deference to a CANSA academic oncologists who would usually attend, and who would benefit and return with knowledge.

CANSA hosted an annual general meeting with the media in attendance, and this was the opportunity to take her down. Lorna, my former PA fed me the inside story. By now the rumour had spread that I was going to intervene and Gamildien, was concerned that I would put my legal training to good use and intercede. She decided she would play the disgruntled former employee card with the media when I attended, except I never attended the report back.

Instead, I had someone there asking questions concerning corruption based on the information Lorna was feeding me.

Gamildien didn't know where these questions were coming? And she didn't know where classified information claiming fraud was coming from either. She would turn to Lorna asking her to go and destroy documents, only for Lorna to inform me and for this to be revealed to the press.

I made front page of the Sunday Times (and other papers), where the bold headline on the front page quoting me screamed 'OBSCENE'.

Gamildien called it disgruntled employees, admitting that she was being paid on a commission basis, something that had never previously been revealed.

It further transpired that there appeared to be a move towards a new board consisting of certain of her staff members together with some of the old board members, with Gamildien in charge. Clearly no accountability.

Given the negative publicity and that this was public welfare money, the board eventually had no choice but to give Gamildien the boot, although the board let her resign in order for CANSA to save face, but sadly not before Lorna's employment had been terminated after Gamildien had finally figured out what had been going on. Lorna Johnson was the real unsung hero, but her actions cost her job saving CANSA from a scandalous looting.

I subsequently bumped into Meyer at a local supermarket. She said she couldn't remember me. I smiled and said, "*The fat lady has sung.*"

IOL: Row rages about use of Cansa's millions

Published Sep 21, 2005

Barry Cohen, a former chief executive of Cansa, on Tuesday labelled what was going on in the charity "obscene", given the new organisation's boss takes home nearly R1-million a year.

Cohen and other disaffected Cansa members say the organisation is riven by infighting and dissatisfaction, and they believe its funds are being mismanaged.

But Cohen's successor, Niamaat Gamildien, 46, says she was appointed on a fixed-term contract rather than a salary, and was financially compensated under the performance-based terms of her employment.

According to financial statements, of the R64-million which was raised in the last financial year, R7-million went to direct patient care and R31,6-million (just under half) went to salaries for Cansa's 300 employees.

The rest – about R16-million – went to the running costs of the organisation, maintaining vehicles and property, training of volunteers, marketing, advertising, and Cansa's campaign promoting a healthy lifestyle.

Cansa's website (www.cansa.org.za) says it is a fundraising organisation committed to offering "a range of services from education, prevention and advocacy work to facilitating research, treatment, care and support for cancer patients, survivors and their families.

"This includes interim homes for out-of-town patients, support groups and home-based care."

But Cansa's Gauteng Regional Manager, Marc Stiglingh said home-based care was no longer offered in Gauteng.

Gamildien was appointed as head of Cansa, having previously served as provincial director in the Western Cape, who at that time was on a salary package of R240 000 a year, and is said to receive an annual package of more than R900 000, including performance bonuses knowing there was to be an increased allocation from the lottery given that Precious Moloi (Patrice Motsepe's wife) was now chairman, the board having used the race card to take out the previous chairman expert oncologist Georges De Muellenaire.

"I feel that what's happening now is obscene," he said, alluding to the fact that Gamildien was being paid almost three times what he had received.

Another complaint levelled against Cansa was that the organisation had spent R240 000 on employing a company to handle retrenchments over a four-month period. At the same time, a second company had been appointed to handle rebranding of the organisation and was placed on a retainer of R60 000 a month.

Stiglingh said: "So, effectively, you had the organisation paying out over R400 000 on retrenchment and rebranding exercises at a time when they could have rather spent that money on salaries."

Former Cansa employee Sandra Miller confirmed she had seen a R240 000 invoice for the company handling retrenchments.

More money was spent on converting the boardroom at Cansa's national headquarters into new offices for Gamildien, while a lapa was converted into a boardroom.

The disgruntled Cansa members believe the renovations "cost an absolute fortune".

Shirley Ingleby, a Cansa secretary before she quit, said that instead of using the new boardroom, the organisation now used hotels. Cansa was to hold its annual general meeting on Wednesday at The Courtyard Suite Hotel in Rosebank, Johannesburg.

The organisation also paid for Gamildien's golf lessons and membership fees at the exclusive Killarney Golf Course in Johannesburg. But she attended only one lesson," claimed Marc Stiglingh.

Cansa and Gamildien came under fire at the annual general meeting after alleged mis-application and under-application of government money as well as funds that were raised, and Gamildien's apparent autocratic management style had come to light.

Philip Gohl, also a Gauteng regional manager, said questions had been asked for some time about what had happened to millions of rands meant for home care and cancer research.

Accuracy of statements queried

Internal investigations already have been launched into what happened to R17m donated by the National Lottery Fund, as well as R2m donated by the department of social development.

Regional managers also questioned the accuracy of Cansa's financial statements. Cansa spokesperson Martha Molete insisted that the financial statements were approved, but Stighlingh denied this.

"A vote about the statements was on the agenda, but it was removed during the meeting. The statements were not approved by the board and was not discussed."

Can serve on the board?

The board, however, accepted an amendment to Cansa's memorandum of association, which determined that Gamildien, her financial chief Wilhelm de Wet and another senior member of management, Joel Perry, could serve on the board.

Gohl said this was contrary to the Fund-raising Act that stipulated that people in managerial positions were not allowed to serve on the board of a non-profitable business.

Stiglingh said that what the amendment meant, in effect, was that the board was cut down to nine members and that the three management members, along with a number of executive and non-executive directors, basically ruled Cansa.

Cohen and other disaffected Cansa members say the organisation is riven by infighting and dissatisfaction, and they believe its funds are being mismanaged.

Gamildien was appointed as head of Cansa having previously served as provincial director in the Western Cape.

Gamildien took over from Cohen, who at that time was on a salary package of R360 000 a year, and is said to receive an annual package of more than R900 000, including performance bonuses.

The Star newspaper: jillg@star.co.za

Fraud charges laid against Cansa board

Published Sep 23, 2005

Fraud charges have been laid against the board of directors of the Cancer Association of South Africa, but they are fighting back in a war of words.

Association member Marc Stiglingh opened a fraud docket at the Norwood police station in Johannesburg on Thursday.

He alleges that board chairperson Dr Precious Moloi and other board members acted illegally by conducting Cansa's annual meeting in their official capacities, when their own memberships had lapsed.

The Star reported this week that while Cansa had raised R64-million in the past financial year, less than R7-million of this had been allocated to patient care, with just under half being used for salaries.

Published Sep 22, 2005

By Alameen Templeton

More ex-employees slam Cansa 'fat-catism

Disgust at Cansa's management has continued to grow. More former employees have come forward with complaints, and the boss' R900 000-a-year salary is drawing more heat.

The Democratic Alliance said on Wednesday it was alarming that "fat-catism has spread to an organisation with such an outstanding reputation for helping the sick as Cansa".

It drew a comparison between chief executive Niamaat Gamildien's package and President Thabo Mbeki's R1 117 199 annual salary, saying there was no justification for the amount she was paid.

Cansa paid out just R7-million in the last financial year for patient care, although it received more than R64-million in donations.

The non-profit organisation remained adamant on Wednesday that Gamildien's salary was appropriate, saying it was "approved by the board and is in line with market-related salaries for people with her qualifications and experience".

Democratic Alliance spokesperson Dianne Kohler Barnard said a review of all salaries was required and that paid executives' salaries needed to be made public.

"All salaries, including that of the CEO, must be brought into line with what is reasonable for such an organisation," Barnard said.

Barnard, however, said Cansa needed to act quickly and decisively if it was to preserve its reputation and its donor base.

Stiglingh expressed reservations that Wednesday's meeting approved Cansa's board of directors and its remuneration committee, although the members of the two are almost identical.

He also accused the organisation of hobbling the ability of its grassroots organisations – the regional committees – to hold accountable the provincial and national councils.

In the articles of association approved yesterday, the existence of regional councils was made optional, and it has been left to the provincial councils to decide whether they want to keep their lesser cousins.

Current and former employees who approached The Star on condition of anonymity said Cansa's internal management was rotten and they have promised to make public the necessary proof.

Cansa's critics, however, say the malaise of the organisation could prove terminal if some of the current leading lights are not brought to book.

Disgruntled former employees and members of the organisation, which employs 300 people, also complained that Cansa boss Niamaat Gamildien was receiving a package of R900 000.

The Cansa's board produced their own figures and dismissed as unfounded allegations that the organisation was being mismanaged.

Cansa boss quits her R1m job

Dec 23, 2005

Million-rand-a-year Cancer Association of South Africa CEO Niamaat Gamildien has resigned. This comes after a panel was set up to investigate allegations that the association was misusing donor funds.

In late 2005, Gamildien finally resigned.

What was sad, was that Georges de Mûelenaere, the former unpaid chairman, and possibly the foremost oncologist based in Pretoria was forced to resign. I had no doubt Kevin Wakeford was trying to engrain himself with Patrice Motsepe. During the Zondo commission he was named as one of the corrupt persons involved with the BOSASA Watson brothers corrupt enterprise and the evidence was handed over to the police to be taken further. He then resigned from positions he held stating he required time to formulate his defence.

After the entire grubby affair was over, I undertook consultancy work for WWF-SA, Save the Children fund, Give 'n Gain, The Giving

*Nobel Peace Prize: Archbishop Emeritus Desmond Tutu and Barry Cohen
at the launch of 'Give 'n Gain'*

Organisation with Archbishop Emeritus Desmond Tutu[44] as our chairman, and other NPOs while I searched for a new opportunity.

Lesson learnt

The fact that it was an NPO should not make one complacent and trusting where staff are concerned. Money and power usually rise to the top, as does treachery.

Consequences should always be your priority when you have a decision to change the direction of your path. In my case, I lost focus on what I could lose should I not relocate to Johannesburg, at least until I had another alternative.

---

44 **Desmond Tutu** was a South African Anglican bishop and theologian, known for his work as an anti-apartheid and human rights activist. He was Bishop of Johannesburg from 1985 to 1986 and then Archbishop of Cape Town from 1986 to 1996, in both cases being the first black African to hold the position. Theologically, he sought to fuse ideas from black theology with African theology. Tutu, Mandela, and de Klerk were all Nobel Peace Prize recipients.

At my age, not many future CEO opportunities would come my way, certainly not at this level. I was stubborn and proud, too proud even to meet with the trade union when they offered to assist. *Pride cometh before the fall.*

CHAPTER 10
GOLF HALL OF FAME & MUSEUM

GOLF HALL OF FAME & MUSEUM FOUNDERS

Harry Brews
Barry Cohen

HARRY BREWS AWARD

'Selfless contribution and growth of the sport of golf'

2013 Hon. Andrew Mlangeni
2014 Mr. Raymond Ackerman
2015 Mr Sol Kerzner

Life has many twists and turns, and thankfully we tend to gravitate to those challenges which we are passionate about.

After turning around The Golf Alliance which had been losing R250,000 monthly, Mike Wells, the owner, reduced my contracted salary contrary to our verbal agreement to double it if I succeeded. As it turned out he wanted me to resign so that he could give the position to his friend, a car salesman who liked to give orders rather than get his hands dirty. It wasn't long before it was bankrupt.

Moving on, I was fortunate to be asked in 2006 to join Harry Brews to help him build the South African Golf Museum. Brews had been a founder and the financial director of Liberty Life. His father Sid Brews, an eight-times SA Open champion, the last when he was turning 54 when they wheeled him out for another go, three years after his last victory.

Sid's older brother, Jock, was also a four-times SA Open winner. Sid had a surprise in store when converting to Judaism. His mother suddenly revealed that she was Jewish which permeated down to Sid's sons Harry and Roger, the SA Amateur champion, and further the Pappas brothers. A similar occurrence happened with the Henning boys, Harold, Graham, Brian and Allan as their mom

Henning Brothers: Allan, Harold, Brian, Graham

was likewise Jewish.

Harry had won the first world international amateur tournament, winning the University Championship at St. Andrews in 1947. His brother Roger won the SA Amateur the same year Sid won the SA Open for the eight time.

My initial role was to source sponsorship to build the museum. Everyone liked the idea, but no sponsors were forthcoming. I even triumphed in the national FNB Enablis Sunday Times Small Business Challenge: New Business category, but then the prize money which we could have used to help build the museum was reneged on, given that I was 'white' and the winners were supposed to come from the black population. A laptop and some office equipment had to suffice. Welcome to the new South Africa.

However, several entrepreneurs from across the country received much-needed financial support as they became winners of South Africa's largest business plan competition – the R50-million Enablis 'Business Launchpad'.

The competition run by Enablis, the Canadian-based not-for-profit organisation that specialises in supporting entrepreneurs in developing economies, saw over 6,000 entrants submit plans for an entrepreneurial venture across 10 different industries, including technology, tourism and agriculture.

We had to present to a panel of experts. The announcement with the spotlight focusing on you. Quite a dramatic moment like the Oscars.

Bottom line, I was not successful sourcing sponsorship. A 2008 golf day fundraising event at Oubaai brought the voluntary participation of legendary Springbok lock Victor Matfield, Roger Wessels, and two-time US Open winner Retief Goosen.

Retief Goosen & Dave Usendorf 2008

Barry Cohen

As mentioned, I had bought my lovely large Spanish-style dream home in Hout Bay which allowed my children, Rory and Jenna and their friends to run around and have fun. I had been drawing from the bond, and now with the Trust running out of money, I had to make a decision. Walk away or sell the house to build the museum.

By chance my wealthy young cousin, Derek Zackon had just returned from London and came to visit. I happened to mention my dilemma and he instantly jumped in offering to join me in building the museum. This meant I would also be able to pay my bond and keep the house. I was delighted.

Derek and I entered into a contract although at the last minute he included an exit clause. We then had a lot of fun driving from Cape Town to George as we constructed the museum.

It was not to be.

Shortly before the museum was completed, Zackon informed me that he was exercising the exit clause, although he would continue if I allocated 51% to him, and further, that he would not pay anything further towards the balance of the purchase price of his shares.

This meant I was now far too committed and that I would have

Hugh Baiocchi, Duggie Donnely, Vincent Tshabalala, Dale Hayes, Louis Oosthuizen

to sell our family home. His response was *"Too bad, your problem"*. Given he was wealthy and everything had been progressing smoothly it was clearly a power play.

With a heavy heart I rejected his attempted takeover, sold our lovely home, which really hurt, and completed the museum.

165

Meanwhile, Zackon kept trying to get back into the deal, but the house was gone. He had acted dishonourably.

Once again, the wheel turned. Of course, I had agreed to the contract, so I cannot complain, but I never considered the possibility that he would use that to try and gain control of the museum. Then, of course there was his attitude concerning my home. He simply didn't care. So much for relatives and the kindness I had shown him when he was younger. My faith in family was really unravelling.

I continued with Harry who supplied the memorabilia, and I proceeded with the building of the museum. William McIntyre, Hyatt Regency Oubaai's CEO, allocated us a large space downstairs rent free. This was the key. I only wish I had kept that foremost in my mind.

I designed and researched placing interesting information on the wallpaper, and Harry acquired Peter Sauerman's excellent memorabilia collection, whilst I appealed to all our iconic golfers for memorabilia.

Finally, Ivan Meyer, the Western Cape Minister of Cultural Affairs and Sport, opened the museum and we followed it up with a wonderful first Southern Africa Golf Hall of Fame Induction Gala Banquet evening, *'The golf event of the year'*, with iconic golfers in attendance or sending messages of congratulations. Those there included golfers, former world number one, Ernie Els, Mark McNulty, Retief Goosen, Louis Oosthuizen, Dale Hayes, Denis Hutchinson, John Bland, Simon Hobday, Hugh Baiocchi, and former world number two, Sally Little, with messages from former world number one, Nick Price, legendary coach David Leadbetter, world's greatest golfer, Jack Nicklaus and David Frost, whilst also making up the numbers included Johann Rupert, Raymond Ackerman, and my friends winning rugby 2007 world cup winning coach, Jake White,

Lindi & Jake White and Ernie Els

Harold Henning's daughter Hayley accepting his induction, Jenna Cohen,
Allan Henning.

Jenna and Barry Cohen

Sally Little & Johann Rupert

Dale Hayes induction, Harry Brews, Rory Cohen

legendary cricketer Barry Richards, and Bantu Holomisa, as well as Minister Patricia de Lille.

Other than the annual 'Million Dollar' tournaments at Sun City, this was possibly the greatest gathering of iconic golfers, and what a posh banquet.

Each inductee was introduced by a famous golfer or personality, and I was given the honour of inducting my hero, Bobby Locke.

Induction of Arthur D'Arcy "Bobby" Locke

Arthur D'Arcy 'Bobby' Locke ... old "muffin face" ...one of the true stars of the game ... dominated the golfing world during the post-war era. ... he won 38 major tournaments in South Africa, 23 in Europe, and 11 in the U.S.A, including 4 British Opens, and as an 18-year old, he was also the low Amateur at the 1936 Open

Recognised as the greatest putter, and one of the top 20 golfers of the 20th Century.......

In America, in the course of 2 ½ years he played 56, won 11, was 2nd or 3rd in 30, whereupon he was effectively banned because he was too good.... And of course we all know his responses to the jibs concerning his distance off the tee ... "You've got a weak left hand ... But I take your cheques with my right hand" .... and ... "You drive for show... I putt for dough".

Incredibly popular at home, he was the most unlikely golfing star, who hit every shot, pivoting on a sixpence, despite his bulk, with an amazing draw, and that included putting spin onto his putts which curled into the hole. ... and he would study the green, especially around the hole, like he was writing a thesis.

I never saw him putt more than a foot short or a foot long. Of course, he could also fade the ball when it was called for, and then there was that slow.. deliberate.. maddening pace at which he played the game.

And what about his unusual dress .. impeccably turned out in a white shirt, tie, powdered blue cardigan, and his plus-fours, with a white peaked cap. He certainly did not spend much time in the gym, nor on the practice range, and his joviality with everyone

belied a steely determination and concentration ... he would
tell me never to talk to him while he was playing a competitive
round ...

His steely nerve was again in evidence when the 2ⁿᵈ World
War commenced, and he signed up as a bomber pilot flying in
North Africa. Given the war, his amazing international career, in
effect, only last lasted around 12 years before his accident and
partial loss of sight.

But it is also as the man that I remember him, as he took me
under his wings as a 13 year-old, and let me play with him, and
he would fetch me to go and watch him and others compete. After
his round he would give me his Dunlop No. 4 golf balls from his
bag, and there would not be a scratch on them, such was the
amazing crispness with which he hit the ball.....And there were
many evenings I would wait outside the bar at Clovelly where
he would be having a sing-song with the members, before taking
me home.

I am sure that were he standing here tonight, he would look
at all of you ..... MAAASTER .... and with a smile, take out his
ukulele and get you all to sing-along ....

Bobby Locke ...Champion Golfer! .... Wonderful Human-
Being!

Guests were welcomed by a troop of African drummers in
traditional African skins, beating out the rhythm of Africa.

Hayes the 1976 European Tour number one, before he retired
at 29 was the compère together with Dan Nicholl, both comedians,
so it was very funny.

Dale retired having arrived in Caracas with Hugh Baiocchi to
represent South Africa in the World Cup, and after a practice round

only two days later they were given 24-hours to leave the country due to South Africa's apartheid policies. He had had enough.

Dale did everything for free and would continue to attend and compère every year at his expense. It was simply the black-tie golfing dinner of the year which was preceded by the Celebrity Pro-Am.

In all a maximum of 128 guests were present, the tables having been booked out three months in advance, and it continued until 02:00. Timing! Such an event should be over by 23:00. I had learnt a lesson.

In planning the event I had received a quote of more than R1million. Given I never had that sort of money besides it being outrageous, I decided to organise the Pro-Am and Banquet all on my own, from sourcing sponsorship and prizes, to invitations, follow up, and everything related thereto. I have never run that fast during the day ensuring its success, but I was gratified my two young children, Rory and Jenna were there to witness the event and to partake by handing out flowers to the inductee recipients in addition to a framed silver carving of their likeness playing golf, moulded by the outstanding sculptor Simon Shone.

The entire induction was filmed for television (SuperSport, SABC) and received many laughs and plaudits especially when Ernie roasted Tiger Woods following his adultery troubles, and praise was received from every quarter. I felt very special, but despite Hayes urging me to request funding from Johann Rupert, given that his wife was in favour, nothing developed.

The golf sanctioning bodies meanwhile, did not come to the party, and the SA PGA declined to participate. The men and women golf bodies were on our board, and all were requested to increase the club golfer fee by R5 to protect South Africa's golf heritage, but there was no movement there, and only a few members of the

*The golfing greats autographed a photo of **Barry Cohen** competing near Airlie Beach, on the Great Barrier Reef. Autographed messages from Ernie Els, John Bland, Mark McNulty, Retief Goosen, Jake White, Dale Hayes, Denis Hutchinson, Vincent Tshabalala, and the naughty Sally Little*

public visited the museum despite the brilliant memorabilia and interesting exhibits and wallpaper.

As mentioned, the museum was situated downstairs inside the Hyatt Regency Oubaai and was brilliantly laid out such that Hayes stated in his weekly newsletter that it was *"one of the three best kinds of museums of its type in the world",* and I received many letters of support and congratulations.

For a while we still hoped that Rupert (and then Gary Player) would sponsor, but, alas, it was not to be. With Harry passing on in 2010 I took over the funding and operational aspect as no one stepped in to assist.

Our board consisted of the men and women amateur golf bodies, Springbok golfer Dorian Wharton-Hood, golf historian Peter Sauerman, Harry Brews, Sally Little, Sir Rupert Gull, and me.

The SA PGA declined to participate even though it was primarily their golfers who were inducted into the Southern Africa Golf Hall of Fame. You must wonder why?

After the 2009 induction I received a complaint that besides Papwa Sewgolum there was no representation of people of colour. Harry and I agreed and persuaded our board to introduce an additional category, namely 'disadvantage' as recognition of the challenges those of colour had to face under the apartheid regime.

Subsequently in 2010 Harry, Sally, Peter and I were in favour of inducting Vincent Tshabalala, the 1976 French Open winner and 4-time SA Non-European Open champion (in the era of Papwa and Ismail Chowglay). This nomination received huge opposition from all the other induction committee members. In fact, I also received a call from Grant Wilson, the Sunshine Tour CEO, stating that Rupert was dissatisfied with this inductee selection given the fact that Tshabalala had written a letter to the Minister of Sport, Steve Tshwete complaining that the PGA and Rupert were not taking care of black professionals and favouring the white and overseas players.

It was outrageous yet we were forced to compromise by also inducting Richard Mogoerane and Theo Manyama. Clearly their contribution came nowhere near the accomplishments of Tshabalala, Cox Hlapo or Chowglay.

This set-in motion my research into black golf given that there were no records other than some commentary on the SA Amateur Golf website, some of which was even misleading and incorrect. Fortunately, I had access to the best golf library in the country at the SA National Library in Cape Town.

Research is a lot of fun. New stories came to light concerning both white and black golfers and administrators, and I looked forward to this daily research at the National Library and night-time scouring the golf records while also bringing up my two young children, fetching and carrying, and burning the midnight oil.

Soon I had compiled a record of all prominent golfers, amateur and professional, from Kenya, Uganda, Tanganyika, Southern (Zimbabwe) and Northern (Zambia) Rhodesia, South West Africa (Namibia), Swaziland (Eswatini), and Mozambique, but finding information on golfers of colour was far more challenging.

Once completed I managed to tell their story on a special subset of wallpaper. It was the story of caddies, bush-golf, TPA Non-European tour, victories, Papwa Sewgolum, and then there was Lewis Chitengwa beating Tiger Woods for the world junior title and winning the SA Amateur.

Players such as Joe Dlamini (Swaziland), Lewis Chitengwa (Zimbabwe), Vincent Tshabalala, Chowglay, Simon 'Cox' Hlapo,

Richard Mogoerane, and administrators Peter Louw and Theo Manyama were selected for induction. And there were others such as Ramnath 'Bambata' Boodhun, the father of black golf playing in the 1929 British Open, Lewis Muridzo from Zimbabwe, and Edward Johnson-Sedibe playing likewise in 1959 in The Open, William Manie in 1960, and Lawrence Buthelezi qualifying in 1970.

Papwa Sewgolum was inducted in 2009 together with the likes of major winners Bobby Locke, Gary Player, Nick Price, Ernie Els, Retief Goosen and Sally Little. Sewgolum's story and achievements despite apartheid, his banning and passport suspension are remarkable and probably led to me writing a well-received book about him in later years.

Left-handed Ismail Chowglay with Papwa Sewgolum both reverse grip, looking on.

Source: Selvan Naidoo (1860 Heritage Centre) & Compleat Golfer

GOLF **HALL OF** FAME

Here's a toast to
Ismail Chowglay

By Barry Cohen

PHOTOGRAPHS: SUPPLIED

IT IS THE SEASON OF CHEER, WHEN WE REMEMBER OLD FRIENDS, and I would like to take this opportunity to reminisce about South Africa's best left-handed golfer, Ismail Chowglay.

Arguably the second best golfer of colour who strode our fairways, Ismail was built like a rake. He stood more than six feet tall (in today's terms, 1.82m), often wore a hat and, boy, could he play!

During the 1960s and '70s, there were many other notable non-white players, such as the Lendis brothers, Percy and 'Hitman' Stan (who you definitely did not want to meet on a dark night), Richard Mogoerane, Vincent Tshabalala, Abe van Rooyen and Wally Johannisen. Although all of them won some professional non-white tournaments (those were the good old bad old days, remember?), they were not quite in the same league as Ismail and his contemporary, Papwa Sewgolum.

Between the two of them, they dominated during the '60s and '70s, winning numerous titles, including the SA Non-White Open. In fact, their combined reputation was such that they often played exhibition games with Gary Player and Harold Henning – and frequently beat them!

Ismail only once toured overseas, playing in the British Open, where he made the cut. Unfortunately, no sponsors came forward to support his foreign adventure and he was denied the opportunity to prove himself in the international arena.

Both Ismail and the right-handed Papwa used the unorthodox reverse grip

FORTY THREE | Oubaai Issue No. 5

But sadly Harry Brews whom I really liked and enjoyed visiting at his home at the Erinvale Golf Estate succumbed to cancer. The Hall of Fame was his idea. I was merely along for the expensive ride.

Funny how this all started … I returned after living abroad, only to discover that my friend, Ismail Chowglay, had passed-on in relative obscurity and poverty, and seemed forgotten by the local golf world, despite probably being Papwa's major opponent in the 60's and 70's, which led to a 'Letter of the Month' written to Compleat Golfer, where the editor, Brandon de Kock contacted me to say that he never knew about Ismail, and that only after he asked the older generation did he appreciate who he was.

Well the Museum is built!

At the outset I approached the South African Golf Association for assistance, and the President at the time, Neil Khunhardt, told me that they had been approached many times for such a project, and that it could not be done. Imagine my delight a few months ago when Neil contacted me, and asked if he could donate some memorabilia to the museum.

South Africa now had a heritage museum of golf which they can be very proud, and where the legacy of those who have contributed will now live on ....

Black-tie inductions attended by the who's who were held annually initially at Heralds Bay, Hyatt Regency Oubaai near George, later

2010 Vincent Tshabalala's induction into the Southern Africa Golf Hall of Fame: Barry Cohen, Hugh Baiocchi, Vincent Tshabalala, Sally Little, Dale Hayes, Cobie le Grange, John Bland

also in Johannesburg (which I found difficult to organise from Cape Town) and Cape Town, with 120 – 130 in attendance covered by SuperSport and other television stations as well as golf magazine and newspapers. Dale Hayes, assisted by Sally Little now co-compered each event.

Our Pro-Am had better fields than some of the Sunshine Tour events. It was incredible. Some like Bobby Cole, Fulton Allem, and Denis Watson flew in from overseas, and others like Retief Goosen, Louis Oosthuizen, Roger Wessels, Gavan Leveson also participated, as well as numerous Springbok amateur golfers.

Around 2014 BMW came on board as our induction sponsor, and the following year Mercedes-Benz signed a three-year sponsorship deal including the museum. Up to this point the museum was at best simply breaking even and somehow, I found ways to make a small living.

Many interesting stories emanated from these inductions. Zimbabwean Denis Watson who was second on the 1984 PGA money list and runner-up by 1-shot in the US Open, but while eating dinner on a lovely seaside deck of a Plettenberg Bay restaurant, regaled how he was penalised two-shots for waiting 15-seconds, and not the 10-seconds as stipulated by the rules for his ball to drop into the hole. This was despite that he had consulted with the rules official who gave him permission to wait the extra time as the ball appeared to be moving, and in fact fell into the hole.

This two-shot penalty was then changed to a one-shot penalty the following year, but one has to wonder what the impact of Watson winning the US Open would have had on his career, instead of the headline 'Watson who?' in reference to Tom Watson and finishing number 1 (not number 2) on the order of merit money list for 1984.

Bobby Locke who won 9 SA Opens (in nine attempts) prior to

his accident also came up for discussion. His career was shorter than Gary Player's as he volunteered as a pilot during WW2. Given that he was unbeatable in the USA from 1949–1951 winning 15 PGA titles before they banned him. The reason given was that he had not attended a US PGA event when he was on the sea sailing to England to defend his British Open title, a title which he won four times before his railway crossing accident in 1958 where he basically lost the sight of his one eye.

Denis Hutchinson was adamant that he was South Africa's best golfer, the GOAT, better than Gary Player. Clearly this is subjective, but he certainly was the most popular with the fans although Ernie Els would later rival him in this regard.

A young Bobby Cole who hit the ball prodigious distances despite his thin lean build, got to play with one of his heroes, Sam Snead in the Masters. Hole after hole Snead strode to the furthest ball only to find it was Cole's. It wasn't long before Snead turned to Cole as they were waiting to tee off on a par-5 and told him how he used to cut the corner over the trees. Cole took up the challenge but didn't clear the trees, after which Snead turned to him with a grin and added that the trees were still young and much smaller in those days.

One of the more moving inductions was Lewis Chitengwa[45] as his brother and sisters joined their parents in flying down from

---

45   **Lewis Chitengwa** Zimbabean, won the 1993 World Junior Championship beating the defending champion Tiger Woods. The following year, 1994, he beat Rory Sabbatini and Tim Clark on his way to winning the South African Amateur Match-Play championship. He featured prominently on the American university circuit and was playing on the Canadian Tour, preparing himself for a tilt at the PGA Tour when he died of a rare form of meningitist. Nick Price, the former world number 1 stated his protegé would surely have won a major.

Zimbabwe including his father, the legendary Lewis Muridzo[46], Zimbabwe's first black professional and coach par excellence having assisted two world number ones, Nick Price and Vijay Singh, and his children including Lewis.

Lewis was a prodigious talent having won the 1993 SA Amateur beating Rory Sabbatini along the way. He was the first man of colour to win this title, but when he arrived at the event, he was told to enter through the caddy enclosure as no person of colour was good enough to play in this event. The year before he was the first person from outside the USA to win the World Junior Open beating the defending champion, a certain Tiger Woods.

He subsequently enrolled at a US University where he was the star of the golf team once again beating Tiger Woods. A protégé of Nick Price, he then went onto the Canadian Tour in anticipation of following in Woods's footsteps onto the US Tour. Having just returned from a visit to his family in rural Zimbabwe and while playing on the Canadian Tour he was suddenly taken ill, and the following day passed away from a rare form of meningitis aged only 26. Nick Price saw him as a future major winner.

Andrew Mlangeni[47] was one of the Mandela Gang of Five sentenced to 27-years on Robben Island in the Rivonia Treason trial,

---

46 **Lewis Muridzo,** the first Zimbabwean professional of colour to play in white tournaments locally and abroad. He also coached his son Lewis Chitengwa, and many other champions, whilst assisting Vija Singh and Nick Price.

47 **Andrew Mokete Mlangeni** was a South African political activist and anti-apartheid campaigner who, along with Nelson Mandela and others, was imprisoned after the Rivonia Trial, and sentenced to life imprisonment on Robben Island. He was released from prison in October 1989 after having served 26 years of his life sentence. Mlangeni served as a member of parliament for the ANC from 1994 – 1999 & 2009 – 2014. He was a close friend of Nelson Mandela and spoke at Mandela's memorial service.

Barry Cohen presenting Andrew Mlangeni with the Harry Brews award

originally a caddie, received a special award for his contribution to golf, and regaled how he had found a golf ball on Robben Island and hid it under his bed to remind him that one day he would be free and able to play golf again.

Rory Cohen, Honourable Andrew Mlangeni, Barry Cohen

I was especially honoured to spend an afternoon with him together with my son, Rory, and he explained how they played chess through their tiny cell bars on Robben Island by calling out the moves which were then relayed up the line. There seemed no bitterness after 27 years in jail. I wasn't even scratching the surface, but I felt very special to be in the presence of someone who had contributed so much to the country.

He followed in the footsteps of Raymond Ackerman for his contribution to golf by opening Clovelly Country Club to members of all races in 1976.

This endeavour went relatively unnoticed until the Southern Africa Golf Hall of Fame awarded Raymond Ackerman the 'Harry Brews award' in 2014 for his selfless contribution to the betterment of golf.

The story goes that he went to see John Vorster, a keen golfer with the bushy eyebrows, and informed him that he was opening the club to all races whereupon Connie Mulder thundered: *"Over my dead body"*. Vorster ordered Mulder out of his office and then engaged with Ackerman telling him that *"if 87% of the members agree"* (an arbitrary figure) the club could open its doors to all. Most members (93%) agreed. This led the way for FW de Klerk[48], three months later, the new Minister of Sport, to allow all sports clubs to decide

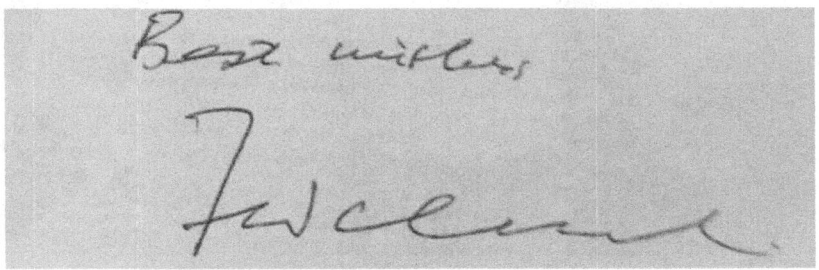

---

48 **Frederik Willem de Klerk**, served as state president of South Africa from 1989 to 1994 and as deputy president 1994 – 1996. As South Africa's last head of state from the era of white-minority rule. Ideologically a conservative and an economic liberal, he freed imprisoned anti-apartheid activists such as Nelson Mandela. He also dismantled South Africa's nuclear weapons program. He received the Nobel Peace Prize for dismantling apartheid and bringing universal suffrage.

By 1979 all the leading players of colour in the Western Cape, such as Stan and Percy Lendis (1963 WP Non-European Open champion), Wally Johannsen, Albert Hess, Moses Mooi, a young 'Slamming' Sammy Daniels, Carl Mentoor, and Abie van Rooyen (WP Non-European Open winner 1970, 2nd '71), were all playing league for Clovelly, whilst Moses Mooi became the first golfer of colour to be selected for a South African Provincial white team when he was selected to play for the WP 'B' team.

Subsequently Ackerman donated this very valuable real estate to the members of Clovelly, and furthermore, set up the 'Raymond Ackerman Golf Academy' which takes disadvantaged children straight from extremely poor communities, who have never played golf, and assists them daily at the club with their school work, teaching them to play golf, and enables certain students to study further at university.

Raymond Ackerman, Mrs van Heerden, President F.W. De Klerk, Barry Cohen

whether to open their clubs to members of colour.

This was to have sequel at a dinner for Ackerman, the chairman of Clovelly CC, to celebrate this opening of the club to all races, where I was invited to sit with former President de Klerk at the main table. I can't say I took to de Klerk whom I found quite dour, cold, and disengaging.

These stories rolled on, like how Cobie le Grange won the Australian Masters beating Jack Nicklaus in his prime and ranked 15th in the world. He built up clubhead speed (which determines distance) by practicing swinging into old car tyres.

Perhaps the most amazing story is that of Retief Waltman, heir apparent to Gary Player. Retief's hero was Ben Hogan, and consequently he wore a peaked white cap. By the age of 24 he had won two SA Opens in the Locke-Player era. The second of which he won by beating the legendary Papwa Sewgolum by a stroke. A year later having already played in two Masters and also having won seven provincial titles, he simply gave away his clubs aged 25 and entered the ministry. He was a prolific talent but his religious calling clearly gave him more satisfaction.

"Papwa" Sewgolum's story is also engaging. He was a South African professional golfer of ethnic Indian origin, who carved a niche for himself in golfing folklore when he became the first golfer of colour to win a provincial open in South Africa. He became a symbol of the sports boycott movement when pictures of him receiving his trophy outdoors in the rain were published across the world: due to apartheid, he was not allowed to enter the clubhouse. Durban-born, December 1929 in a shack to a mother going blind, illiterate, and whose father passed on when he was 10 such that he and his brother had to look for work to support the family as Indian girls did not work. At 13 he became a caddy winning the Natal Indian Open in 1945 aged 16. It was such an astonishing feat such that there was reluctance to give him the trophy.

He then followed it up winning the Natal Non-European title five times before he was discovered at 27 by Graham Wulff who had just invented Oil of Olay.

As Sewgolum was refused permission to play in SA tournaments, Wulff decided to enter him into the British Open. The next hurdle was how to get there as people of colour could not easily fly on SAA. Not bothered, Wulff bought a four-seater Piper aircraft and flew it through Africa to England, a thousand kilometres at a time. Papwa, now 29, then incredibly qualified as one of 60 participants for The Open which was won by Gary Player.

Playing in only his second 'white' tournament, the 1959 Dutch Open, Papwa beat the best of Europe, where a crowd estimated to be 100,000, mostly Indians, lined the Durban streets in welcome.

Sewgolum's win barely raised a ripple with the white press, but it raised a red flag with the authorities.

At last India could also celebrate an international sporting hero. He won the Dutch Open the following year, and three-times in four attempts. Now the pressure was on the South African apartheid authorities. Finally, he was allowed to compete in the 1963 Natal Open, but was granted no practice rounds and no clubhouse entry.

Against all odds he beat a top field to win the Natal Open, with the SABC pulling the plug on the radio commentary over the last few holes. Thousands of Indians followed him in round the course, but petty apartheid legislation determined he had to accept his trophy outside the clubhouse.

Whilst receiving his trophy it started to rain with the white golfers (other than Bobby Verwey) comfortably ensconced inside the clubhouse. With streaks of lightning, photos of this injustice flashed around the world outraging India, and leading Prime Minister Nehru to have SA banned from the 1964 Rome Olympics. Papwa was now inadvertently the figurehead of the anti-apartheid sports' movement, despite being A-apolitical.

Runner-up in the SA Open and with 10 victories in the SA Non-European Open from 1960 – 1970 with his only real challenger being Clovelly caddy-master left-handed Ismail Chowglay. Chowglay, who also played "reverse gripped", also playing with a reverse grip, was rated better than Papwa in 1962.

Papwa was once again invited to play in the 1965 Natal Open, but this time he would face the world number 1, Gary Player, who was to win the US Open later that year, as well as Harold Henning.

Head-to-head they faced off, Gary and Papwa's army of supporters cheering them on, with neither giving an inch. It was

Papwa, a man of colour, and contrary to the superiority of the apartheid white-man policies triumphed. Within two weeks mixed sporting galleries were banned.

After beating Player again, Papwa was banned from all South African white tournaments, finally after coming second in the 1966 Dutch Open and a successful appearance as their new iconic sporting hero in the India Open, the government took away his passport. This prevented him from traveling abroad. He died aged 49 alcoholic and destitute.

Questions were raised why Player did not do more to assist Papwa given his regular games with Vorster. In his biographies during the 1960s and 70s Player repeatedly stated he was a supporter of apartheid, but he did later support Vincent Tshabalala.

Tshabalala's story was equally remarkable. A truck driver, he started playing golf at 20. Hooked, he would rush to his bush golf course as soon as his shift had ended. In 1974 Gary Player sponsored him to a trip to Europe and the USA but he never made a single cut, despite being an incredible long-iron player, which he also played with the reverse grip used by both Papwa and Chowglay.

Then in June 1976, again sponsored by Player, he went to play in the French Open. Pulling his own cart in the final round due to the lack of finance he triumphed against a top field including Seve Ballesteros.

Upon his return he was instantly selected to partner Gary Player in the World Cup but refused. This was just prior to the 1976 school uprising in Soweto where he lived, but more than that, he said he was only 13th on the money order of merit list, only allowed to play in certain white tournament, nor was he allowed to be a member of the SA PGA. Clearly this was a political selection and Brian Henning heading the SA PGA had Vincent immediately suspended from playing in further tournaments.

Years later, on the practice tee at the 2010 induction event Vincent met Sally Little where he pulled out a cutting from his wallet showing Sally winning the US Women's Open in 1976 which he said inspired him to win.

Gary Player attended the 2018 induction at the V&A Waterfront, Cape Town and when walking through the museum prior to his formal induction explained how his greatest tournament was actually the 1972 US Open where he finished runner-up to Raymond Floyd, but where he was heckled, had ice thrown at him and golf balls rolled between his legs when putting.

Stories kept emerging from the woodwork. Then there's Swaziland's Joe Dlamini who grew up playing on bush golf courses, and it was only in his thirties, when he was permitted to play on the Sunshine Tour circuit and where he became a regular winner. We tracked Joe down and the Swaziland Senator Mike Temple brought Joe to the Induction. Much gaiety followed.

As mentioned, Hayes was the compère at each event, assisted by Sally Little. Not only did he have great knowledge and an amazing pedigree, but he is genuinely funny. He was the leading money winner on the European tour in 1976 at the age of 24 and retired in 1979 at 27 after arriving in Brazil to play in the World Cup together with Hugh Baiocchi, only to be given 24 hours the following day after a practise round to leave the country due to South Africa's apartheid policies. By now Dale, was the "'voice of golf'" in South Africa and formed a fine commentating pair with Denis Hutchinson. Our friendship went back many years to when we played junior golf, but Dale was always the star.

This was followed at the Compleat Golfer annual dinner in Johannesburg. Simon Turck phoned to confirm that I would be attending, but I declined. He tried again, but again I declined, so finally he let the cat out of the bag, that out of the blue I was selected to receive the award for the *2012 'Greatest Contribution to the SA Golf Industry'* with Charl Schwartzel who had just won 'The Masters' receiving the 'Greatest Contribution to Golf' award.

Compleat Golfer Annual Awards Dinner

JOHANNESBURG (21 February 2012) – Compleat Golfer hosted the 20th edition if its Annual Awards Dinner brought to you by Mercedes-Benz at Randpark Golf Club on Monday, 20 February 2012.

With MC Dale Hayes in fine form behind the microphone, the evening recognised the excellent performances of those in the industry in 2011 and was enjoyed by the Who's Who of the South African golfing industry.

Nick Price was awarded the Contribution to Golf award in recognition of his services to golf in Southern Africa, while Southern Africa Golf Hall of Fame Barry Cohen founder was given the Contribution to the Golf Industry award.

Other award winners on the night included 2011 Masters winner Charl Schwartzel for Compleat Golfer's Player of the Year and Ashleigh Simon (later Buhai) for the Comeback of the Year.

Ernie Els was awarded the Newsmaker of the Year award for his induction into the World Golf Hall of Fame in 2011.

All the winners

- *Compleat Golfer Greatest Contribution to the Golf Industry **Barry Cohen***
- *Compleat Golfer Golfer of the Year Charl Schwartzel*
- *Compleat Golfer Newsmaker of the Year Ernie Els*
- *Compleat Golfer Comeback of the Year Ashleigh Simon*
- *Compleat Golfer Contribution to Golf Nick Price*
- *Mercedes-Benz Mover of the Year George Coetzee*
- *WGSA Ladies Amateur Golfer of the Year Kim Williams*
- *WPGA Achiever of the Year Caryn Louw*
- *SAGA Men's Amateur Golfer of the Year Brandon Stone*

My Compleat Golfer Award acceptance spe ech

What a journey … when I returned to South Africa from abroad I was distressed to find that my friend Ismail Chowglay had died in such poverty that I was motivated to write a letter to the magazine. The editor, Brandon de Kock, phoned and inform me that he had not previously heard of 'Papwa's' main rival and South Africa's best left-handed golfer.

At the same time, Bobby Locke's wife, Mary, had sold off his memorabilia and later committed suicide with her daughter, so when I was asked by the Sid

Brews Golf Development Trust to launch a Hall of Fame, the time was right and it fitted in with my passion.

However I never contemplated the financial downturn late 2008, when not only did sponsorship dry up, but the Trust ran out of funds, such that I agreed to take over the financial responsibility.

Although there has been no financial support from the corporate sector, we received support from all the golf bodies, iconic golfers, and public sector, such that with both Harry Brews and my help, the museum was recently opened.

When I first approached the SAGA, Neil Khunhardt, then President, told me that this was a project which could not be done, so recently I was pleasantly surprised when he donated memorabilia to the museum.

Those of you who have seen the museum have been gobsmacked, as it appears to have exceeded all expectations insofar as the story it tells, memorabilia displayed, interactivity, library, and of course the hall of fame........ good thing I never visited a golf museum....

We have many plans for the future development of the Hall of Fame brand, and I urge corporates to touch base with me to discuss the various opportunities. Likewise, we are involving all club golfers in the museum, so please feel free to chat with me... or simply loan or donate memorabilia to the museum.

It has been a difficult road, one person, one PC, one designer, one researcher with help from Peter Sauerman, no fax, no scanner — shows what can be done — but it did cost us our home. However, in the words of Jackie Mercer: 'Winners are not quitters, and quitters are not winners'.........

So to Compleat Golfer, thank you very much for this award ... it is hugely appreciated!

As mentioned, golfers flew in from all over the world like Fulton Allem, Bobby Cole, Denis Watson, Hugh Baiocchi, Joe Dlamini, the Henning Family, Lewis Chitengwa family, and Mark McNulty. And if they could not attend, others sent messages like Jack Nicklaus who sent congratulations to Gary Player, David Leadbetter, Nick Price for Mark McNulty, and David Frost. One of the most enjoyable inductions was Johann Rupert inducting Ernie Els and his response, only because they were both so funny.

Numerous ministers such as Tokozile Xasa, Bantu Holomisa, and Patricia de Lille attended and it was a who's who from the business community including Sol Kerzner, Thabang Moropa, Lew Geffen, Fred Worner, Raymond and Jonathan Ackerman, Johann Rupert, Adrian Gardiner, Dorian Wharton-Hood and the like.

Museum collectables continued to be donated including items such as the 1965 Canada Cup (from Harold Henning). However, once again as the saying goes, nothing lasts forever.

Selvin Naidoo, the marketing manager for vehicles at Mercedes Benz informed me after an excellent Oubaai event that Mercedes-Benz would not be renewing their three-year sizeable sponsorship unless I relocated it to the Cape Town V&A Waterfront where Mercedes-Benz were one of the key sponsors.

I asked Selvin for an agreement, but he explained that the sponsorship only became due in June. However, sponsorship allocations for the next period could only be concluded from September. He reassured me that everything would proceed.

Given that the museum was struggling financially, I was once again blinded by greed and the desire to keep Mercedes as our sponsor as it would cover both my salary and any future operational shortfall. Fred Haremza, my retail partner and I also thought we would also do a roaring business selling autographed memorabilia.

Remember I was paying no rent at Oubaai, and in fact, when Haremza and I met with the Hyatt Regency hotel, the MD offered not only reconfirmed there was no rental payable on the premises leased, but they would even pay us R1000 p.m. simply to keep us there. Clearly, we were an attraction for them.

I really missed Harry Brews' calm judgement, and truly I should have also discussed this with Peter Sauerman given the time and money both gentlemen had invested in the Oubaai museum. I trusted Selvin, we had a good relationship, Mercedes had been generous, and he had guaranteed this conditional sponsorship renewal.

What was I thinking! We had a spacious museum at Ernie Els's signature club, beautifully set out. It was paid for, and I had invested a lot of money in building it. It was also a wonderful excuse for me and the children to regularly drive there from Cape Town during the school holidays to enjoy the Garden Route and the luxury facilities the hotel and golf club provided.

No, I knew better, and again my gambling nature reared its face. Stupid, stupid, stupid! You only move once a renewal contract has been signed, but premises had become available at the V&A Waterfront, something which rarely occurred, and during June with the help of others we uplifted the museum and rebuilt it at the Waterfront by the Clock Tower using the rest of my money and more.

David Green, the Waterfront MD, warned me that museums do not make money, but after discussion with the Springbok Rugby Museum I was confident we could make a go of it, and further that we would be able to cover our R70,000 per month rent.

Before David would approve the lease, he requested confirmation from Selvin that Mercedes-Benz would be renewing their sponsorship. Selvin did just that, and a lease was drafted.

But there were complications. Gary Player was only available at a given date in July to open the museum and attend the induction where he was to be formally inducted. He had only one demand, namely that I fly him and his kind wife, Vivienne in a private charter plane from their farm, and accommodate them and some of his guests at the hotel. To do this I had to borrow money. I don't think anyone realised that I was paying everything out of my own pocket. He subsequently sent me a book of his with a lovely inscription.

The premises offered were a lot smaller than Oubaai so it was a matter of squeezing everything in. At the opening the weather was an omen as it poured and was very cold. Gary Player, the Minister of Sport Tokazile Xasa, and Sally Little cut the ribbon. Gary was very complimentary. Unfortunately, he never viewed the improved version at the Oubaai museum.

Many dignitaries attended the opening and the Induction at the Radisson Waterfront hotel. It was once again an outstanding event which included a beautiful young lady playing the violin in a bubble in the forecourt. It simply could not have been better organised if I may say so myself, sponsored again by Mercedes-Benz, and with Gary Player, Sol Kerzner, Raymond Ackerman, Johann Rupert, Minister of Sport, Bantu Holomisa, Patricia de Lille, Fulton Allem, John Bland, Sally Little, Dale Hayes, Denis Hutchinson, and many others with video messages from a number of parties including Jack Nicklaus.

Again, I organised everything on my own from home. I thought I had pulled off the impossible and that Mercedes had received the media attention and branding they deserved from television, print, and those attendees. Then the cracks appeared!

Naidoo started getting cold feet. He told me he was being directed by head office in Germany to move away from sponsoring golf, which sounded like a fabrication. He then agreed to a one-year sponsorship. With all (and more) of my savings having gone into relocating and building the museum I gave a sigh of relief. Then

SPECTACULAR HALL OF FAME OPENING IN CAPE TOWN

Johann Rupert, Gary Player, Hugh Baiocchi

Gary Player

he reneged on this offer, and now offered to sponsor the following induction event, but later withdrew this offer leaving me with my R70 ,000 monthly rental.

As it turned out Naidoo effectively destroyed the South African golf heritage museum and all the goodwill and memorabilia already sourced by not being honest with me and David Green from the outset. This was even more curious as Hugh Baiocchi sent me a message after the event stating that he played with Kobus van Zyl, to whom Naidoo reported to, and *"he is very enthusiastic that Mercedes are involved with the Hall of Fame"*. A blight on his employer Mercedes-Benz.

Karkloof Safari Spa: Rory, Jenna and some of the game

Suddenly I was staring down a black hole. Could I return to Oubaai? They had leased the premises. And having just spent over R2m I could not afford to rebuild or re-locate again.

Meanwhile my great friend, Fred Worner, the owner of Karkloof Safari Spa, the resort below Hilton College at Howick stepped into the breach paying a substantial portion of the rental, and repeatedly inviting us to holiday at the resort (it was incredible teaming with game), until the Waterfront head office objected to his branding on the outside of the building.

I just could not win. The expected number of visitors based on the nearby Springbok Rugby Museum did not materialise, and neither did the retail store do the expected numbers. In fact, not one piece of memorabilia sold!

With Karkloof Safari Spa's sponsorship of R50,000 pm coming to an end, and delays in the Waterfront opening their international cruise terminal which would bring potential visitors to the golf museum as they had to walk past us, things were very bleak especially as I had already spent all my money and could no longer pay rent. Had I had sunk as low as I could go?

I found myself depressed. Just traveling to the Waterfront was an effort, whilst phone calls kept coming. How bad could things get?

Meanwhile, I offered the new body, Golf RSA, which had taken over as the overall golfing body, all my research on white and black golf but was rebuffed. During all these years neither Golf RSA nor the Sunshine Tour had bothered to invite me to one golf event or dinner, nor thank me for what I had done.

But then, unbeknownst to us, Covid-19 was coming.

Lessons learnt

Trusting my young cousin was a wake-up call, especially as I had assisted him growing up. It is the same old story, once a clause giving the option to withdraw had been entered into the contract, I should have planned ahead knowing that there was a risk and that I could lose my home. The fact that I simply did not contemplate this was stupid and only added to my discomfort.

The trust issue was to again rear its head with Mercedes-Benz. How could I have not waited until we had entered into a contract before relocating to the V&A Waterfront. Player had given me two dates when he could attend, so why was I in such a hurry?

How stupid could you be? And to destroy everything Harry Brews, Peter Sauerman and others had helped me build.

Sometimes it is worth taking a step backwards no matter what others are encouraging. They are not taking the risk. Discuss it with a team or someone not personally engaged who can give an objective opinion, rather than succumb to gambling. The pain that comes with depression and shame is simply not worth it. Think ahead as the grass is most definitely not always greener on the other side.

CHAPTER 11
COVID-19: Angels on my shoulder

As Jackie Mercer said: "quitters are not winners and winners are not quitters."

2019 was a pivotal year.

I was in a severe depression wanting to give up on life, owing at least R350 000, unable to work, and certainly unable to get a job at my advanced upper-sixties age, and having to support my two children who were still at school.

Creditors scoffed at the thought that I couldn't pay them, but were patient, until with help from overseas friends I was able to settle some accounts.

I could no longer afford our home rental, and following a nasty spat between my daughter and a foul-mouthed Polish bully of a landlady, we agreed to depart.

Then **Covid-19 struck**. I mean this was the really bad one. People were dying! Everyone was scared to go out unless necessary. Seniors even had a special early morning time to shop, and masks were in short supply.

The V&A Waterfront became a ghost of a shopping centre. Other than staff it was abandoned. Promotions did not help. Sales were nil. Unable to pay the bills it was time to close the museum.

I literally couldn't bear the pain seeing all my money I had spent on the Oubaai museum and now the V&A Waterfront Museum go up in smoke, and all I could do was place the memorabilia in storage. It was a dreadful death. All the people who had assisted me. I had let down everyone.

Our prayers were answered as my young friend, **David Allen**, who had lived a while with me at Airlie Beach, and whose brother, Michael, had been my good friend, came to the rescue. He owned a palatial eleven-room Spanish-style mansion overlooking Hout Bay beach and the bay. It had a dream view with a spectacular garden situated at the top of the mountain. The house was unoccupied. We could stay there for a substantially reduced rent until it was sold. What was originally intended to last only three months became five years.

The house was on the market at R26m, would we kindly stay there until it was sold? Of course, we would.

Day in-and-out I was applying for work. Clearly there were no jobs. We were restricted to the house. What could I do with little money? Years ago, I had painted and exhibited, should I start painting again?

Motivation was so difficult, but I had to get out of bed for the kids and force myself to go for a jog up the mountain.

While looking for work, I realised there was so much information I had found concerning 'Black Golf', and after receiving no interest from the golf bodies, and realising that no one other than myself would ever record this 'lost' history, why not write a book on black golf?

It had never been done. What else was I going to do. I still had access to the only record of all the golf magazines since 1926. I recalled eagerly reading these tournament results on a Tuesday in the local newspaper, with names such as Polly November, Abe van Rooyen, Ismail Chowglay, Percy and Stan Lendis, Wally Johannson, Albert Hess, and Papwa Sewgolum jumping off the pages.

I would get on with my research and writing until it was time to collect the kids from school. I would read the golf historian R.G. Fall's[49], research and information through the night looking for anything to do with a reference to black golf.

I had never written before (I made an attempt to write an adventure novel in 1980), never thought I could write, but slowly the book came together. I loved the research and really could wait to get going in the morning. Eventually it was time to publish *'Blazing the Trail' (90 years of black golf)*.

The book not only detailed the legacy of black golf since 1876 but told many stories about golfers and administrators that had been lost in the mist of time, such as Ramnath 'Bambata' Boodhun, the father of black golf, Peter Louw who kept golf alive organising tournaments and building bush courses. Or, Hlapo the champion before Papwa, Johnson-Sedibe, Ismail Chowglay and Papwa Sewgolum, Edward Johnson-Sedibe playing in The Open 1959, Lawrence Buthelezi, Vincent Tshabalala, Joe Dlamini, Theo Manyama, Richard Mogoerane, Lewis Muridzo and Lewis Chitengwa, as well as many others, as well as the advent of black golf clubs, the TPA tour, and the results of most of the TPA tour events. It was a real compendium of black golf together with photos. Amazing stories of triumphs against all odds. Already heroes to millions but unknown to white readers.

I also included a subset rating all Southern Africa golfers including 'black' golfers who had never previously been included in any ranking, as if they simply did not exist.

I didn't just write this story out of the goodness of my heart – I applied for and was given a lottery grant. The money was to sustain

---

49 **R.G. Fall** whom we inducted into the Golf Hall of Fame in 2009 was the editor of the monthly SA Golf magazine from 1926 – 60s, and it's these surviving newspaper records, including black golf and golfers such as Papwa Sewgolum that were bound yearly, and the museum had the only two copies.

It was unheard of for anybody to beat Tiger at that time, then people started to discover he already had a really impressive career in Zimbabwe and traveling around the world.
— Mike Moraghan
Executive Director at Connecticut State Golf Association

Lewis Chitengwa
University of Virginia Alumnus and Junior Golf Champion

us for quite some time, while the project focussed me and drew me out of my depression.

Given that I am ADD, I become fanatical when proceeding with a project I enjoy. Nothing else matters or gets in the way. Hours were spent doing research and I scoured the old newspapers which were fascinating, especially the Indian and Black newspapers, which information, as a white during apartheid, I had never seen.

Oh, what joy, now I couldn't wait to get up in the morning and get going.

What was remarkable is that I was not an author, rather I saw myself as a researcher. After many months, eventually it was finished. The manuscript was over 400 pages and I was eager to get it published. Today I cringe as clearly it could have been substantially improved and re-edited.

Praise was received from every corner with overseas reviewers (see addendum) stating how South Africa should be so grateful to me for recording this history.

Having by-passed publishers after I was initially told it was such a niche market book that there would be no interest, I self-published, but the book did not sell well. This was a setback as I printed 1000 copies in the expectation of sales.

Much like the books on the history of rugby and cricket, *'Blazing the Trail'* was to be the bible on black golf, and the chain Exclusive Books featured it as one of their July "top 20 local author promotion" where I joined panels exploring sport books. What fun talking about something I knew and with the book featured at all their branches.

And that's where it stayed, on their featured section. I was excited when I saw the numbers ordered by them and by the other bookshops, and I thought we had a smash hit. Slowly they were returned unsold. Clearly golf is a niche market and black golf even more niche.

National Museum Publications

"Greens, roughs and Blacks": The establishment of a black South African golfing tradition before World War II – BY HENDRIK SNYDERS JULY 8, 2019

An important recent addition to this small collection is the book by Barry Cohen (2019) which specifically looks at 90 years of black golf in Southern Africa. This publication, in comparison to its predecessors, aims to tell a much wider story. Although its contextualisation is limited, it has finally assisted in foregrounding the history of a long golfing tradition amongst black South Africans. Its major strength lies in the fact that it puts faces to the names of those that have both played and administered the game.

I then decided to re-write the book I wrote many years before with the help of famous British playwriter, Geraldine Aron. It was a Wilbur Smith-type book set at the gold fields 1895 – 1900. An adventure based on fact, bushveld, gold, the Uitlander uprising and Jameson raid, and eventually the Anglo-Boer war, and which was entitled '*Let the Storm Burst*'.

It was such an interesting book and really fun to research. I was sure it would be a hit. But hardly a copy sold. Lucky I only printed 50 copies to see the offtake.

I later realised there was a further book emanating from the first, namely the story of Papwa Sewgolum, the famous golfer of colour banned by the apartheid government.

Two books had already been written about Papwa, but I realised that I not only had played golf at a high level, I had in fact watched Papwa teaming up with Ismail Chowglay to play Gary Player and

Vincent Thabalala at the new Kuilsriver GC, having just opened for people of colour, which they won 2/1, and that much of the information stated as fact was incorrect, and the actual description of these tournaments was totally inadequate.

These two books had been written by non-golfers and were trying to discuss apartheid and politics as well as Indian home life rather than doing the research and focussing also on his amazing talent – golf!

I applied for and received another smaller grant and again I was off and running. Papwa was so interesting and this time there were plenty of reports locally in the Indian newspapers and abroad.

More and more information came from everywhere, and by now I knew what I was looking for and how to make it interesting. I still regarded myself simply a technician putting together events and outcomes.

There were so many stories in-between not just about Papwa but about those parties who touched his life. I lived the story, and life at least levelled out.

Not so!

One day while driving to our last Induction event at Plettenberg Bay which was being held in conjunction with the SA Senior Open, I received a call from Grant Wilson, still the CEO of the Sunshine Tour *(never once was I invited to a SAPGA event or tournament though they were invited to my events and their members inducted at my expense. Actually, for this reason I never invited Grant to the magnificent 2017 banquet, and upset, he wanted to know why)* enquiring whether I still owned the SA Golf Museum and the Hall of Fame project.

Given that Johann Rupert pulled the Sunshine Tour strings and having unsuccessfully appealed for their assistance a number of times, I suspected that they were now hoping to jump in and secure the project for free.

I told him that it was mothballed in storage and we were looking for new premises but that it was for sale. We finally entered into some serious negotiations with Golf RSA.

Negotiations dragged on, and I was later told their inactivity was because they were unsure whether to trust me despite my having put time, effort and money for the betterment of golf in the country. Be that as it may, they finally acquired the project paying me a fair price given that the project was languishing.

What with repaying debts I had incurred and paying for our trip to Australia the money earned from the sale of the museum and its contents was soon frittered away. Easy come easy go.

My best friend in Cape Town, **Harry Trisos**, approached me with the idea of investing into an English Language school in Vietnam. I was very hesitant and declined.

He continued to knock at the door, informing me he had various substantial investors, and eventually I succumbed to the tune of R500, 000 after I received a positive report from a competent Price Waterhouse Coopers (PWC) accountant who had visited and invested in the project. Later I was to discover her investment was actually in lieu of work to be performed, no cash. Harry then got my former girlfriend to invest R1,25m.

I got cold feet as the money was for the kids' education and I realised I had been wrong and requested the return of the investment. Harry agreed stating he could easily sell off these shares, but he had now reached the zenith of those investing, and I had to hold my breath and hope the project succeeded.

While setting up this operation in Vietnam and changing its

original structure Harry kept reverting appealing for small loans to help the home situation such that before I realised that I had stupidly loaned a total of R120,000.

Now with Covid-19, Vietnam ordered all in-person learning establishments to close for the next 18 months. Just as the doors to our investment had opened, now we had to close.

Nevertheless, with an investment of R3,2m we thought there should be enough to ride out the storm as far as rent was concerned. This was not the case and Harry closed the project. Investors couldn't understand what had happened to the money and equipment, and responses from Harry only led to further questions.

I understood that he could never have predicted Covid, and I suppose I was actually cross with myself for initially agreeing to the loan and putting the children's education at risk.

Eventually I was to ask for the refund of my small loans, but only received a scurrilous legal letter from Harry's associate and attorney, Tony Buirski, stating that Harry had loaned nothing and insulting me insofar as I was not practicing as an attorney, the same elderly attorney who the Law Society had previously struck off the roll. I couldn't believe it so I twice queried this with Harry, given that he must've signed it off, without a response. I then suggested we meet for coffee, after all this was my best friend in SA, again no response.

I then took one of the loans to the Small Claims court to test the situation. The day before the trial this same attorney who had stated Harry owed me nothing, asked if we could settle with payments, staggering them over a period of time. A coffee was proposed to clear the air, but nothing eventuated. A small payment was made, nothing further, and I simply dropped the case and the subject. I was saddened and angry that such a strong friendship and trust of 50 years could be broken.

CHAPTER 12

FILM 'PAPWA'

I hoped my Papwa book *'Blazing the Trail'* would sell well, but being wiser I only self-published 500 copies, but before I had it printed, I sent the manuscript abroad to those who had reviewed my previous book on black golf, and I will always be grateful to Roger

McStravick[50] in London. No sooner had he received it than he sent it on to his friend Carolyn McMaster[51], who founded CHAOS a Film Company based in Calgary, Canada. Being a golf fan, she was looking to make a film on Old Tom Morris, but as Roger explained, Morris was born, won a number of British Opens and died, nothing too dramatic.

A few days later I received a call from Carolyn to the effect that she was interested in optioning the book as she thought it had Academy Award potential.

I informed her about the other two Papwa books and that both had been optioned locally for a film. The first book was by Judge Christopher Nicholson in 2005 followed by Maxine Case in 2017 but that didn't deter her, and in no time at all we had signed a contract, possibly the last unknown golf story.

What a turn around. Clearly there was an angel on my shoulder. I was so excited. This was way beyond anything I had dreamed about, and to also be engaged as a consultant on this possible film.

Carolyn engaged a professional scriptwriter using my initial draft film script as a precedent. Some good ideas there. A second chance, and I could dream about the future and after so many years, not having to worry whether there would be sufficient money to cover the bills for next month. I still can't, nay will not let myself believe it until the film is announced but isn't it exciting!

---

50   **Roger McStravick**: Double winner of USGA's Herbert Warren Wind Book Award 2015, 2020 and British Golf Collectors' Society Murdoch Medal

51   **Carolyn McMaster** is a Canadian film producer and president of CHAOS a film company. In 2022 Carolyn produced the Walter Hill western Dead for a Dollar starring Christoph Waltz, Willem Dafoe, Rachel Brosnahan and Benjamin Bratt. Dead for a Dollar premiered at the Venice International Film Festival.

I don't know why it is happening to me, and it looks like my kids, Rory and Jenna, will be provided for when I am no longer here.

Both film companies had approached me as the authority to act as an advisor when (and if) their films were produced. Both companies were looking at a $5 million budgets and had no real reputation as a major feature film producer.

I then informed Rajen Sewshanker (Papwa's son), who agreed to support this initiative as Rafiq Samsodien whom he was supporting hoping to also make a Papwa film, had spent six years trying to source funding and hadn't yet come up with anything.

Rafiq was incensed stating that this was a South African apartheid story, and had to be filmed by those who suffered, but he was open to chat. Consequently, Carolyn made contact.

But by this stage, Rajen had changed his mind, denying he had confirmed his support for our project, and threw his family's weight behind Rafiq. Clearly Rafiq had chatted with him, but it surprised me that he would lie to my face, especially as we had always gotten along well in the past, and that he had written the foreword for my Papwa book.

Carolyn then offered Rafiq the role as assistant producer of the movie, which Rafiq dismissed out-of-hand. He wanted to be in charge and vowed to source his projected $5 million budget, way short of Carolyn's likely $15 million. He felt I was betraying him and informed me that he had a likely sponsor in Johannesburg, but to-date there has been no word. He ranted stating that this was a film about a black man during apartheid and could only be understood and made by a person of colour and not an overseas production.

Given my financial situation I had no choice but to take Carolyn's option fee, and had made no commitment to Rafiq other than I was open to advise him if he wanted. I had done my part. He had received an offer to be involved and had turned it down.

Meanwhile, the other party who was looking to also make a similar film on Papwa, David Selvin, who had taken an option on the first book written about Papwa in 2005, had yet to source the funds, but he was more pragmatic and made overtures about working together with Carolyn. He wanted both his wife Catherine's involvement as director and their film script to be used.

Carolyn explained that high-profile actors follow the reputation of the director, and she had her doubts concerning Catherine, also I felt David's script was not only factually incorrect but opened Carolyn to potential litigation from Mark Player (Gary's son). She turned him down

The wheel of life had turned again.

Launch of Jeff van Rooyen's book 'Unshackled': Tarina Patel (Bollywood actress), Barry Cohen and Aimee

Meanwhile I was approached by **Jeff van Rooye**n, a 'mixed-race' gentleman around my age, at the time the longest serving financial director of Pick 'n Pay and one of the original parties involved in the transition from apartheid to the new democracy, to assist him with his biography.

He'd bought '*Blazing the Trail*' when playing at Clovelly and what I wrote resonated with him. We met at his club, Country Club Johannesburg and had lunch. We got along famously, a kindred spirit, and he was to lead me into a new direction.

He asked me to fly up again to Johannesburg so he could show me the township where he grew up. He had achieved so much in his life, and I was excited to be drawn into a world I knew very little about.

Upon my return from Johannesburg, my son Rory started noticing some peculiarities in my behaviour and finally contacted my childhood close friend, Dr Jeffrey Melmed, who persuaded me to go to the hospital for a check-up.

It took a few hours to persuade me, meanwhile I was drinking lots of sugary liquid. To make him happy we went to hospital, even stopping on the way to buy a drink, where they told me my sugar level had spiked at 200 and not the normal 5: *"It was lucky you came in as two days later and you would be in a coma."*

Next thing I know, I'm in a hospital ward. Yes, I had Covid and this had brought on type 2 diabetes, such that for the next few days they were pumping me with insulin. When I spoke on my mobile, I could hear myself gasping while chatting and this must have concerned some folks. I was now in hospital receiving oxygen, with the hospital full of covid patients and the death rate rising daily.

No visitors were allowed, and I found myself in a ward with three other elderly patients, two of whom were clearly off their rockers, and I was told were unlikely to survive. They were shouting during the day and screaming at night, oh what joy, but I simply kept quiet for the first five days. Then the one gentleman pulled off his nappy and started urinating on the floor and I went ballistic. They clearly got a fright, and I was asked to calm down.

I managed three hours sleep nightly, given that I was woken for insulin about six times a day. Rory apparently was in tears at

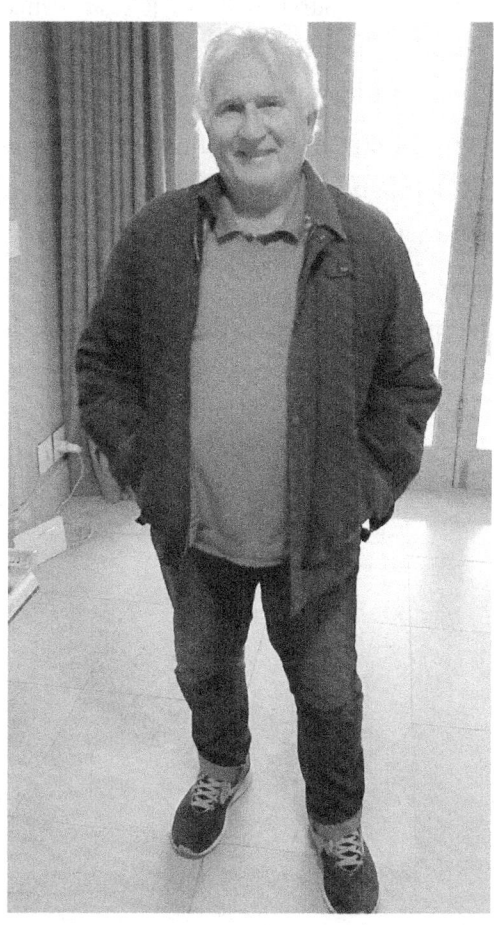

Back home thinner after covid and hospital

home, whilst I listened to wonderful music on Spotify using my headphones.

During the night I would get up, sit in my corner, and read. When not reading I would daydream about the film and going to the Academy Awards with my nephew Sasha, now based in LA working as a major feature film editor. A week later I was allowed to go home.

I didn't know what caused the diabetes, but I guess that was as a result of all the ice cream, marshmallows, jelly and chocolates. Hmm, I have a sweet tooth. Now I had to change my diet. Hospital had one good outcome as I lost around 12 kilos. What a joy!

Type-2 diabetes wasn't the only thing brought on by Covid, as now I noticed my left hand (spreading to my right hand) was at times shaking quite badly, an essential tremor. Badly enough to cause me to stop playing golf

Then I was personally assisting Jeff with his biography 'Unshackled' which became a best seller and introducing him to the audience at talks attended by over 100 leading guests at a time.

CHAPTER 13

Becoming an AUTHOR

Roundabout this time I bumped into my old law friend, **Hannes Wessels** with whom I had sat at law lectures and played rugby. Hannes was from what was then Rhodesia, a big-time hunter and former war hero who had become a well-known author, specifically Zimbabwe war books. We decided to collaborate with our writing, and he asked me to first co-write Mike West's story, a super soldier. This was followed by an amazing Australian legal story, 'The Boys from Bulawayo', concerning two former Rhodesians who had inadvertently got themselves into trouble with the law in Australia for helping two mothers protect their children from sexual abuse.

Hannes is a much better author than I am, and I have learnt from him. Then he asked me to assist with the rewriting of the Sam Levy biography. Rhodesia/Zimbabwe's 7th wealthiest tycoon.

Meanwhile Carolyn flew into Johannesburg for meetings and we followed it up with a trip down to Durban. Around this time, I was also approached by Tarina Patel, a well-known Bollywood and South African actress. She wanted to be part of the Papwa production and indicated she could also assist by bringing finance to the table.

Tarina flew down to Cape Town where we got along like a house on fire. If only I was 30 years younger... She is quite famous, especially in India, and very wealthy, her husband being Iqbal Sharma, who was caught up in the R25m Nulane Gupta affair, but like all Gupta-related trials, the defence cocked it up.

Anyway, she and Carolyn got on well, and Carolyn, Jeff, and I had a wonderful dinner with around twelve other international guests from throughout Africa in their palatial home. It was an evening to saviour.

Then it was off to Australia to join Jenna, and try and give her support, with Rory following in February after he completed his BCom degree at Stellenbosch University.

Now Carolyn broke the news, the Canadian funding for the film has been secured. The budget was set around the $12 million mark, and it seemed like we were finally on our way.

Not so fast...It turned out the fellow providing the cash was a bit of a con artist, and she's back to securing the cash. I don't know if it will reach the heady heights of an academy nomination, but it is my long walk to freedom as we will not have to count our pennies when we go shopping. There may be a little over for the pleasures of life.

If I had stayed in Australia and not sold my homes in Airlie Beach and Peregian, Noosa Shire, I would not have wanted for anything in life as these homes are prime and probably worth around A$8-million (Australian) today. Remember my combined bond was

A\$200, 000 (Australian), but I would never have met such interesting people in my life or achieved what I have left behind. Yes, I would have had a lovely fun lifestyle sailing and playing golf. Looking back serves no purpose. I'm here now!

Meanwhile Jeff van Rooyen got me to join his trust, 'Finding the Fair Way', to assist golf caddies to be permanently employed. As it stood, they travel to be at the golf club by around 06:30, hope to get to carry a bag and be remunerated between R150 – 250 (\$10 – 20) and possibly some refreshment after nine-holes, during which time some of them would be the golfers' 'best friend'.

But the moment the game was over, the golfer would retire with the other players to the nineteenth hole and not think about the caddy until their next game.

Some days the caddy would not get a bag, and go home empty-handed. There was no sick leave, holiday or bonus pay, nor a retirement annuity. Yet the golf club advertises them as an added attraction offered by the club to anyone playing at their course.

When Covid-19 hit, clubs were initially closed and, after that, no one wanted to hire caddies for fear of catching Covid such that the caddies and their families went without work and could not even benefit from government allocations.

Clearly this was wrong, and we set about obtaining a legal opinion, which stated that they were permanent employees, and to which the relevant Gauteng Provincial department agreed. Jeff also had a video made highlighting the unfairness of caddies' professional lives.

We then approached GolfRSA but they fobbed us off and tried to have an intermediary look after the caddies for a cut from the caddy purse. We blocked that by getting the caddies to endorse us as their representative.

Then we approached individual golf clubs only for them to blow us off. Slowly this changed as they realised the caddies are actually their responsibility. Clovelly CC once again led the way employing their caddies followed by Royal Johannesburg & Kensington, whilst other clubs are at last talking.

There are approximately 10,000 caddies countrywide. Recognition of their plight will change their and their families lives. In addition, we have aligned the Trust with UNISA to upskill these caddies, for which we secured a grant and a programme, the Golf Caddies' education, training, and development program, such that they can move onto to higher paid jobs within and outside of the club, whilst the OR Tambo Foundation are supporting us with their initiatives. We are slowly making a difference!

Lesson learnt

Don't put off until tomorrow because sometimes tomorrow simply doesn't come. As for writing, we must enter the unknown, and have courage. Maybe we will be laughed at, but at least we tried and achieved something that we thought was impossible. And every now and then an angel sits on our shoulder and we unexpectedly get lucky. When that happens be very grateful and generous.

Back on the horse – My latest books

Hannes Wessels and I decided it was time to part. We were having a few bumps, and quite frankly our interaction was a poor financial decision. No sooner had we agreed to separate, then I was approached by my book distributor, Mark Hackney who offered to assist with the publishing of my next books.

PAPWA: Against all odds, discovered at 27 and taken abroad, he wins the Dutch Open 3 times, 2nd in the SA Open, and wins the Natal Open 2 times beating Gary Player and becoming the figurehead of the anti-apartheid movement only to be banned from playing in white tournaments and had his passport withdrawn.

The Boys from Bulawayo: Two former Rhodesians, help a mother on the run with her twins who were being sexually abused by hiding them for four years. Then they are arrested and the Australian Federal Police throw the book at them' A challenging legal drama: a Family Court order or the rights of the children?

The Cedric Kushner Story: Cedric Kushner broke the mould by following his passion insofar as organising and promoting music bands (the Rolling Stones, Queen, Fleetwood Mac, Doobie Brothers) and boxing (over 300 world title events especially the heavyweights including champions Hasim Rahman and Sugar Shane Mosley)events abroad at the highest level and ignoring the naysayers who look at school reports to gauge potential. We are all good at something. We just have to find our passion. What matters in life and what you achieve and the memories you leave behind. Cedric was such a man.

Of the four titles listed above, *The Boys from Bulawayo* is undoubtedly the most legally contentious. This is because you are not allowed to disclosed the identities of parties or influence the jury before a trial is concluded, and an important trial featured in the book is still in process. So given there is a chance the Australian Federal Police (AFP) might litigate against the publisher and author. I have taken that risk by changing names and only utilising law reports featured in the print media.

But it is *The Cedric Kushner story* I am most excited about. Cedric grew up six doors from me in Muizenberg and was the local legend or a thug depending on your view. His story is incredible and inspiring. Everyone living in Muizenberg knew him, and requests for copies from old friends are pouring in. I'm very honoured to have been able to tell his story.

CHAPTER 14

ROMANCE and lessons learnt

Yin and yang. I always thought I would marry my best friend. When I was in my teens Merle Lifson[52] came to stay with my cousin Hilary,

---

52   **Merle Lifson** played in productions ranging from restoration comedy to street theatre; the classics to musicals, made a TV movie, was in the TV series Valley of the Vines. Performed in Present Laughter (with PACT); The Best Little Whorehouse in Texas (for Des and Dawn Lindberg). Acted in the Space productions Don't Drink the Water, The Incredible Jungle Journey of Fenda Maria, Lysistrata S.A., The Riddle Machine , Edward II and You'll Come To Love Your Sperm Test. For CAPAB she acted in Roulette, Tartuffe, Along Came a Spider, Women Behind Bars (as Mary Eleanor, 1984); for the Baxter in The Fantastical History of a Useless Man and The Cherry Orchard.

She played in the Pieter Toerien Productions The Hollow (1983), the part of Jill Mason in Equus and in Two Into One (1986).

her broken arm in a plaster cast. She was all bones and gangly, but clearly liked me as she gave me three golf balls as a present.

As the years progressed Merlie relocated from Port Elizabeth to Cape Town to study drama and turned into a most beautiful honey blond beauty with very long hair below her knees, and as an actress, into a stage, radio, and television screen princess.

Sometimes we are limited by shyness and not being forward. We were spending time together as close friends. When it was suggested at my cousin's wedding that it was about time we got married, we both half-laughed it off.

1976 Barry Cohen

Then it was studying flat out, and off to New Zealand. When I returned on holiday from Australia in 1986, Merlie wanted me to take her back with me. I didn't as I had now met Liane. Clearly Merlie and I were suited, we were best friends and had similar interests, she would even come with me to watch rugby – but we were often involved with someone else.

I think Merle got tired of waiting for me to make the right move, even though we would slyly look at each other in the company of others.

Eventually it looked like we would finally hook up, but then Renee whom I had been seeing was pregnant, and we got married. I caught Merle's eye at the marriage and saw how difficult it was for her, but she subjugated her feelings and became friends with Renee, after which she met Christian, the love of her life, and they married.

A few years later Christian, who was a wonderful and kind friend, passed on. Merle was devastated. Just prior to my catching Covid-19 we discussed finally sharing a place at Sedgefield.

My cell phone rang. It was Merlie who was phoning to tell me she now had Covid. I told her to go see a doctor, but she said she was talking to two doctors remotely. Having just been in hospital I could empathise and knew it wasn't fun. The thought that she may get worse and pass on flashed through my brain, but then I dismissed it, and we chatted about the possibility of my coming up to see her. At this point I simply had to financially tread water and hope that the film proceeded.

Then the phone rang again, she was in hospital. She didn't want to talk for too long as she was having difficulty breathing. Everything will be alright. I thought again of going up, but from experience, the hospital would not let me visit the Covid ward.

A Facebook page supporting Merle popped up. I couldn't believe how many people were sharing their love and urging her to get better. She was turning the corner, especially when her brother Frank messaged that the hospital said he could visit. I breathed a sigh of relief.

The following day there was a fateful call. I think it was from my cousin to say Merle had passed on. I was in shock. In many ways she was my rock who always believed in me and was there for me. She even worked for me for a time. She was so talented and interesting, patient and giving, and all she wanted was to belong and be loved.

My world cracked a little. That is not to say I in any way negated her strong love for Christian. He understood 'our friendship' and was my good friend. A really special 'buddah', as Merle would call him. I think of her often with love. So many memories, so many images in my mind....

There were others so far in my life such as Angela (Angie) Brown, a North Queensland television presenter producer of children's program *Totally Wild* whom I originally met in Townsville sailing on Southern Cross. She had a cockney accent having spent some time in London, and I was instantly taken by her bubbly personality and her voice.

Embarrassingly I turned to her and commented on her wonderful tan. Turned out her mother was from Thursday Island and father Scottish. Boy did I feel foolish. She just lit up the stars and I invited her to the opening night at the ballet.

No sooner had we arrived than we were surrounded by youngsters requesting her autograph and wanting to talk to her. She seemed so comfortable with her admirers, and clearly her television programme was popular.

Later, she had her film crew stay at my home in Airlie Beach while they filmed Southern Cross. Again, I clammed up, although during the night I watched her sleeping softly. Soon thereafter my difficulties presented themselves.

Angie was very upset when I returned to South Africa and asked me not to go, but I had difficulty confiding in her concerning what had occurred, and anyway, I thought my return would be short-term and told her, so I can't blame her, but I was smitten.

As it was, I did not return and a number of years later I was married. Nevertheless, a few years later, she wanted me to join her on a holiday in Mauritius. I got as far as Johannesburg and turned back. I couldn't betray Renee whom I had married although Angie was also someone I could have married.

I tried to remain in contact with her, but she cut me off. When I returned to Australia with my kids in 2019, I called, but she declined meeting for coffee.

My beautiful wife Renee

There were others like Liane, as well as Fran, Janet, and Deborah, but, although close at the time, they never had those strong feelings for me.

Finally in 1998 lovely Renee and I stopped seeing each other for 10 days. I think this was mutual, and it seemed we would go our own way, only Renee came and informed me she was pregnant. I always wanted children, and we decided to get married.

There was still some reluctance on both our parts, and the day before the wedding, Renee called to say I didn't love her and the wedding was off. In some ways I was relieved but I went round to see her. When I opened her door I got a bucket full of water thrown in my face.

We were married on a Constantia wine farm on the the shortest day of the year, 21 June 1998, and the sun was shining. Was this an omen?

After eight years we knew we were in trouble and sought counselling. Some years later we separated with the kids living with me. However, she contracted serious melanoma and came to live with us while she was undergoing chemotherapy treatment. This is serious, but it has been around 7-8 years and she is presently managing okay. We still 'care and love' each other and remain close friends, and she has come to holiday with us in Australia.

CHAPTER 15
SPONSORSHIP hints to succeed

- Concluding sponsorships is difficult and there are a number of steps required to be successful.

- Plan who you will approach by ascertaining which companies are likely to support your project and who you should be contacting, usually the sponsorship or marketing manager.

- Prepare your presentation in the most professional manner, including a value proposition for whomever you are approaching. That requires you to research what will make the sponsor interested in your proposal. Remember they are only interested in what benefits them, not you.

- Formulate a database wherein you include each approach, response, and any other relevant comments.

- Make sure that you enter into a contract.

- Don't be intimidated. Aim for the stars, you may be surprised. Remember they are only employees.

- Come prepared and be prepared to think on your feet. All you have to do is ask, and who knows, you may succeed.

- Investigate other forms of raising finance such as lottery direct and indirect applications. Direct mail appeals, and other forms of fundraising such as golf events, auctions, and the like. Also remember there are other forms of sponsorship such as media exposure, auction items, and prizes.

- Formulate databases of supporters if that is possible.

Some of the below-the-line sponsorship fundraising I have been involved with include scratch cards, premium-rate telephone, golf and banquet events, lottery applications, national events such as hair shaving and national golf tournaments, as well as newspapers ink-jet number lottery, and fantasy league contests.

Some of the larger above-the-line sponsors I have landed over the years are: Red Cross, raising R35m, BMW one 1-year Hall of Fame and Mercedes-Benz 3-years R3.2m. Karkloof R750k, ABSA R3m and, of course, Lottery applications.

CHAPTER 16

PEOPLE in my life

Strange to realise I have had dinners with Presidents, Nobel Peace Prize winners, Ministers, Sporting legends, and leading Business icons, and that is besides my lifelong friends. Let me try and recall some of these.

Lady Khama

The legendary 'white' wife of Seretse Khama, Botswana's first President invited me to her farmhouse. It was just a normal home, nothing too lavish, with her son Ian Khama hanging around. Little did I realise he would one day also become the president. She was a rather feisty lady, who was not really looking to socialise, but she approved of our Red Cross fundraising scratch card project, although it was not too long before she fired the Botswana Red Cross CEO, Catherine Thupalagye with whom we had an excellent relationship, and who had invited me home where we danced the 'African' way. Something to do about employing family and finances. Funny, but I received a call from Catherine six-months ago after 30 years enquiring about trading opportunities. The voice was the same.

Lady Masire

With Quentimile Masire coming to power as President, his wife took over as the chairlady of the Botswana Red Cross. She was very much a mother figure and was very kind and motherly towards me. I liked her very much and when I went to meet with her at government house, Quentimile was emerging. Seeing me he rushed back inside to put on his jacket.

As previously mentioned, they invited me to a state dinner just as my 18-year-old niece Mandi was arriving in Gaborone from Australia and I immediately took her to the dinner where ministers and ambassadors in traditional robes and attire were present. We were seated at the table with the ministers who all started handing Mandi their calling cards and inviting her to visit. An evening under the stars dancing to the African beat, a night to remember.

Their daughter Matsudiso or Tsidi was particularly friendly taking me around the country and booking me into her father's presidential suites, so unbelievably luxurious with animal skins on the floor and a huge room with a lounge for entertaining. I think she had a bit of a crush on me.

Archbishop Emeritus Desmond Tutu

Winner of the Nobel Peace Prize, and a thorn in the Apartheid government's side while Nelson Mandela was in jail on Robben Island, had the ability to joke with anyone and everyone, such as when we were traveling in an airport bus. He simply resonated goodness and joviality, laughing and joking with all.

Later, I together with four others put together a charity, *The Giving Organisation*, which consisted of fundraising for the seven leading South African charities including CANSA, Child Welfare, and Red Cross, with the Arch as the Chairman. We celebrated the founding with a lavish luncheon. I felt so 'holy' being with him.

General Bantu Holomisa

From the get go, Bantu attended each and every Golf Hall of Fame Induction and did whatever he could to assist. A golf fanatic he is also a great friend. The former deputy Defence Minister in Mandela's cabinet, and chosen heir apparent by Nelson Mandela, he then had the audacity to accuse Minister Stella Sigcau of taking bribes from Sol Kerzner the casino and Sun City magnate. Despite drawing the most votes of any minister in the 1994 elections, the ANC turfed him out, so he formed the United Democratic Party taking total control of the Transkei.

He set up my appointment with then Sport Minister, Fakile Mbalula. The hope was that Mbalula would support the golf museum. The meeting was very business-like, even abrupt and cold. Amazing how this short man presently wields so much influence.

Another time I wanted to give my book 'Blazing the Trail' to President Ramaphosa, another keen golfer playing off a 7-handicap. Bantu set up an invitation to the President's dinner.

Bantu is really an amazing fellow, very bright, funny, and the seeker of truth with a substantial 'honesty' following in South Africa. He would be my choice to lead the country out of its mess.

Mr Bantu Holomisa, MP
President of the United Democratic Movement

Minister Tokozile Xasa

Another interesting Minister of Sport who followed Mbalula, again introduced by Holomisa, who also attended the Induction and who agreed to write the foreword to my initial book on *Papwa* entitled *'Blazing the Trail'*. We got on like a house on fire so much so that she invited my friend Sally Little and I to Parliament to hear her giving her opening speech and where we were warmly welcomed as honoured guests

She then invited us to a private dinner with her family. She was

Barry Cohen, Dr Divan Serfontein (Springbok), Sally Little

so funny as after a few glasses she got totally paralytic such that she wasn't able to stand up.

Sally Little

Sally and I are best friends from the age of 13 coming up through Junior Prentice golf ranks. Given our close friendship I was asked a few times whether we were an item. Anyway, Sally, a two-time major winner on the LPGA tour and former world number 2 had to go to the USA to receive another award and captain the Rest of the World Senior team against the USA, so she asked me to attend the Sports Award dinner and receive an award in her place from temporary President Kgalema Mothlanthe.

What a lovely man who was our temporary President when chatting with him, the only ANC member to challenge the corrupt President Zuma from within the ANC party at their elections.

Attending the dinner was also 'the blade runner', Oscar Pistorius and his then girlfriend Reeva Steenkamp, who was sentenced soon thereafter to jail for subsequently shooting and killing Reeva. They seemed such a happy couple, and Rajen also received an award for his dad, Papwa.

Minister Patricia de Lille

De Lille and Sally had formed a close bond. Originally head of her own Western Cape party with a substantial following she joined the DA but later fell out with them launching her own 'Good' party and then being asked to join the government as Minister (presently the Minister of Tourism).

When Renee came to these dinners, she would suddenly get up and depart by 21:00 leaving the kids with me while I was organising the running of the event. Being at our table in 2010, and as the kids were young, I had her 'baby-sit' Rory and Jenna. Oh, the life of a minister...

Raymond Ackerman

Raymond Ackerman, the founder of Pick 'n Pay supermarket chain, and formerly an excellent golfer until Denis Hutchinson beat him 10/8 in the SA Amateur.

He gifted Clovelly CC to the members after he had succeeded in opening it to all races.

A soft spoken, kind generous man, nevertheless driven to succeed not only in business but when we played social golf. Very loyal to the country he was known to care for his employees and help with transformation in the country.

Raymond was a regular at the Inductions and we decided to introduce a category, 'Contribution to Golf', with Raymond the first recipient for this gesture. Clovelly then hosted a dinner for Raymond where he insisted that I sat at the main table with President de Klerk.

I tried to engage with F.W., but he was cold, abrupt, and very 'Afrikaans'. I'm such an easy going fellow, but not that night. Still a historic moment for me.

So many other people of note, my friend Jenny married Johnny Clegg, who was Trevor Zabow's brother-in-law for a time. My friend Jake White winner as coach of the 2007 Rugby World Cup with the Springboks, and others.

Gary Player invited Sally and I to play in the Gary Player Invitational. Afterwards, he arrived at the dinner, already in his 80s but dancing and looking like a pop star from the 60s dressed in black, just like his hero in the cowboy movies. Clearly his healthy eating habits and exercise through the years have paid off.

I have mixed feelings about Gary. Given his worldwide celebrity status, just like a Hollywood star, it must be challenging for him and he throws up an invisible bubble around him. He must wonder who his true friends are. Clearly his son Mark is presently not one of those, and certainly I found Mark difficult to deal with and who kept me away from his dad. It was only thanks to Sally and Dale Hayes that I got to spend time with Gary.

Hal Shaper

Of all these celebrities, the one I enjoyed the most was my aunt's brother, **Hal Shaper**[53], South Africa's most famous lyricist and

---

53   Hal Shaper lyricist from Muizenberg. "Softly, As I Leave You" (1962) was his first hit, initially released by Matt Monro and in the US by Shirley Bassey. His work was released by well-known artists including Frank Sinatra, Elvis Presley, David Bowie, Bing Crosby, Elvis Presley, Barbra Streisand (for whom he wrote "Martina"), Petula Clark ("My Friend the Sea"), Jack Jones ("The Years of My Youth"), Val Doonican ("The Mysterious People"), Lena Horne, Bobby Darin and Richard Anthony. He further created and published approximately 60 movie soundtracks for films such as The Go-Between (1971), Papillon (1973), The Boys from Brazil (1978), and First Blood (1982). For these, he won the Ivor Novello award multiple times. He also wrote various musicals for the theatre including two award-winning shows: Treasure Island and Great Expectations.

songwriter, having hosted the Baftas four times, numerous number hits like *'Softly as I leave you'*, and five West End musicals. He referred to me as his cousin, and not only were we golf partners, but he had me accompany him to various celebrity opening nights. He was larger than life, good looking raconteur who lit up the room and a fun person to be with.

We started an international cyberclub and its wonderful every weekend we childhood friends starting from when we were 5 years at school, going to our rugby, cricket, and dance parties still find things to chat about. A band of unbroken friendship who emerge to welcome you whenever you travel to their part of the world. We chat about friends, family and particularly sport and politics.

There have many others with whom I came into contact with besides those already mentioned including famous Vidal Sassoon (with Hal), Springboks CJ van Der Linde, Divan Sefontein, Victor Matfield, John Villet (a cancer survivor after 25 years), and Joost van der Westhuizen, cricketers Robin Jackman (England) one of the really great guys. (*I had previously worked with his wife*), Hugh Tayfield going through a rough time in Australia, and disgraced SA Protea captain Hansie Cronje[54] who seemed like a nice bloke at the time shortly before he was exposed, and so many others.

In 2022 I was invited to a dinner for prominent Western Province golfers from 1967 – 1984 where I was singled out and thanked by

---

54 **Hansie Cronje** was captain of the South Africa national cricket team in the 1990s. A right-handed all-rounder, as captain Cronje led his team to victory in 27 Test matches and 99 One Day Internationals. Cronje also led South Africa to win the 1998 ICC KnockOut Trophy, the only major ICC title the country has won to date. In the 1998 ICC KnockOut Trophy Final, Cronje played a major role with the bat with his 61 not out, leading the team to victory by 4 wickets. He was voted the 11th-greatest South African in 2004 despite having been banned from cricket for life due to his role in a match-fixing scandal.

OB Barber (who organised the dinner) for attending. What a thrill! It was wonderful to see my old junior golf competitors and many stories flowed with the beer, like how I felt intimidated playing Bakkies Loubser in the under-15 semi-finals with his dad following and advising him.

CHAPTER 17

My BELIEFS and the PURPOSE of life

1. I believe in honesty, generosity, and kindness whether rich or poor, and if possible, to help uplift those less fortunate, especially when times are tough. Listening is half the solution.

2. There is other life in the universe, what form it takes may well be very different to life as we know it. Wars in certain galaxies is highly likely, but Earth being so puny is unlikely to hold much interest to conquering intelligence

3. There are definitely invisible webs that bind us, like a spiders web, and there are 'angels' looking out for us. A high invisible life form. I don't know, although I would like to think so, but I definitely believe in the afterlife, but what form it takes is a mystery, and likewise for what purpose our paths keep crossing. Why that is I don't know. Maybe it has something to do with a past existence

4. Some of us fall exactly under our predicted horoscope on a month-to-month basis. I am an Aquarian. Again, I cannot explain it.

5. I like to think we should behave and learn from nature and how animals live with their young in family packs until they are old enough to venture off with their own pack

6. What is our purpose? I have no clue.

7. Evil can be equated to the desire for power, greed, and money. There is so much more to living. It is what we achieve with our lives that define us and creates satisfaction. If you risk nothing, you get nothing.

8. There are some things which you cannot mend, some hurt which has gone too far. Mostly you can forgive but not forget.

9. As my former best friend, Marty Gluck once told me; We must all walk our own path.

10. There are definitely other wave lengths and means of communication, we have simply not discovered them, although there are a few individuals who have touched on these unknown realms. In my case, every few months for a week, a month, or years, I may recall someone I haven't communicated with for thirty years, and immediately I hear from them, or I have dreams which in the morning prove to be true, whilst likewise terrifying predications have come to pass. (The Bible talks about prophets.)

What is exciting, is that there is so much to learn, and mankind will develop progressively at a rapid pace, especially with the help of modern technology, such that the world will be a very different place in a hundred years. Telepathy and intuition may be the way forward.

The PURPOSE of life

I don't know the purpose of life, and maybe that will be discovered at some stage of our evolution given that only a tiny fraction on our brain is presently utilised, but I do have some theories.

The bible as a historical book informs us of dreams the 'ancient' people like Abraham, Isaac, Moses, Noah and Jesus had. It would be foolish to discount such dreams. Likewise, there have always been 'dreaming' people around the world like the aboriginal folk, and Native Americans, especially after taking some form of hallucinating drug.

What is interesting with the bible is that these dreams seem to refer primarily to a select people of the Jewish faith. Is there a reason other than maybe the bible was written by Jews? I do believe in dreams as I have experienced them at the most unusual times.

When I was young my sister, Lindsay and I would on the odd occasion attend séance readings at our home together with my folks and their séance circle. There was a regular crowd headed by Max Frank (a prominent attorney), who headed the Cape Town Psychic Club, and their medium, Matfield, an uneducated man from a poor area (Woodstock) would enter into a trance when spirit 'voices' came through him in different accents and even languages.

We would see cones flying around the room, and I recall my uncle being told that his mom was gravely ill, such that they rushed off. She had had a stroke, or when a voice came through in German, being a missing WW1 pilot, the son of one of the attendees, informing us where they could find his remains in a forest. A search party subsequently found the downed aircraft and remains.

Some of the regular voices talking to us were Ronnie, Ayer, Ingram, Bertram, Walter, Mickey and Boudrain. Even though there were folk who had passed and with whom you wanted to talk to, you could never do this. We were told upon passing you move through different future levels. Some stay longer at these levels as they still have lessons to learn.

I recall Boudrain, one of these was purportedly a 'bad wicked' pharaoh (or from his court), and the manner in which he spoke and what he said was way above me, but so real, whilst Mickey was a young cockney worker selling newspapers on the streets of London during the 1920s and had been run over by a bus. He was very funny.

We know there are people who can telepathically send messages, see things others cannot see, or make cutlery bend (like Uri Geller). During one séance I was informed that I had the gift to be a medium but that I would have to be trained.

To me this was probably nonsense, but many strange things have happened to me.

People have their own take on the 'spirit world', and it is not for me to say if it is real or not, I was young, maybe 13 or 14, but I believe in it. After the séance the adults would give Matfield some money and a lift home. He appeared very exhausted.

Dreams

I have had three or four very unusual dreams when I least expected it. One was when I dreamt about my former best friend Marty with whom I was inseparable, like a younger brother even though we were only a few months apart. We were at school together, cubs, and played rugby and golf, whilst his mom was like a second mom. We had lost touch after traveling through Europe at 21 after he relocated to the USA.

Thirty years later I awoke with a start. My wife asked me what was wrong, and I told her I had dreamt my friend's mom who passed from cancer had told me that he was sick. I then proceeded to track him down, but he said he was fine. However, his wife insisted he had a check-up where they found he was in the early stages of cancer and it was resolved.

Another time I awoke with a start during the night, explained my dream to my wife. She asked what did it mean? I explained that my aunt's friend, Babette had died. The next morning, we heard on the news that she had been attacked, raped and murdered.

I also seemed to go through stages, it may be monthly, yearly or every few years, when I receive phone calls, which emanated from folk I hadn't spoken with ten, twenty, thirty years ago, and I answer the phone greeting them by name before they even speak. I just know who it is, likewise sometimes I know what people will be saying before they say it. There is simply no way of knowing when this will repeatedly occur.

Talk about Synchronicity. Recently I was walking along a deserted beach at New Brighton, about 20 minutes from Byron Bay, Australia, and a fluffy curly dog comes up to me, which I pat. Along comes a woman, enquires whether the dog knows me as it does not usually approach people. We get to talking, she's an Australian originally from Switzerland, but mentions that her father lives in Zimbabwe. It so happens she lives four doors from me. I happen to mention my writing partner, Hannes Wessels is also from there and her mouth drops open. Her dad and Hannes are friends. He then visits and we watch rugby together when I realise Hannes and I are selling his books.

Then I receive a strange email from my late mom's cousin that there is a family gathering in Israel for his 90th, and that he has come across a photo of Michael Lipow who lives in Australia but looks exactly like my grandfather Chaim. Does anyone know him? Is he part of the family?

It so happens, Michael and I started school together at SACS and we tend to chat every fortnight. How strange is that!

One of the strangest incidents was when traveling with my girlfriend to the Kuranda Market above Cairns, around 1990 where I had my fortune read. I drew out the 'death' card, and I was informed that there was to be great changes in my life and that I would travel far away. At that stage I laughed it off. I was in semi-retirement and everything was going great.

Shortly after returning to my home to Airlie Beach my friends relocated to Sydney, my romantic relationship ended, the man who had bought me out and was paying me off went bankrupt, and I had to sell my two wonderful homes, and I ended up returning to

South Africa on holiday and staying for over 30 years.

At the same time my sister has had my yearly horoscope made up for me on a number of occasions on a month-to-month basis, my birthday being in the month of Aquarius. Blow me down if 95% of what I am told will happen on a monthly basis, actually happens. I seem to fall exactly under my projected star sign.

What do I conclude from all of this?

- As our brain and the ability to think develops we will understand so much more.

- There are invisible threads throughout the universe linking our intelligence. We can't at this stage control them, but that will come. These threads have been expanding as the universe expands.

- We know that we can't travel faster than light in our present molecular make-up, which is why when light in the form of stars enter black holes the light disappears, but both thought[55] and imagination travels faster than light. So could black holes be a vortex to travel from one dimension to another, or is there another form of time travel vortex?

What is exciting are the discoveries being made by the James Webb telescope and just last week, the realisation that there was a gigantic black hole soon after the 'Big Bang' theory when there was only a similar amount of mass around, causing scientists to reconsider the entire Big Bang theory.

As we and all matter are made up of molecules is it possible that these molecules may reconnect and be put back together after

---

55 Thought is finer than ether, the medium of electricity. Thoughts excel light in speed. While light travels at the rate of 186,000 miles per second, thoughts virtually travel in no time. Thought is finer than ether, the medium of electricity.

traveling through such a vortex.

Does this explain the invisible threads linking some of us? It is quite incredible how we can bump into someone we are connected to in the least obvious place thousands of miles away multiple times when the odds are millions-to-one.

My cousin on holiday in Thailand met someone new who out-of-the blue mentioned he knew me.

I am not the only one who has experienced these anomalies, and I predict as the brain unravels, thought and imaginations, together with understanding, inter alia black holes will see us travel to the furthest galaxies along these invisible threads.

CHAPTER 18

LESSONS LEARNT including depression

- When making decisions concerning a change, whatever that may be, try to look ahead and consider all possible consequences.

- Whenever you enter into a business decision, be it to sell something, loan money, or enter into a business relationship, always conclude an agreement. This may be a simple or complex agreement, but often over a period of time the memory plays tricks, or maybe you both have differing ideas of what you have agreed.

- In any negotiations you will probably find the most ground given or changes agreed are at the last moment. Be careful about this.

- Sometimes in a negotiation, it is better to say nothing and wait until the other party speaks, however long it takes.

- You grow up in a society with certain views and values. Maybe you've only interacted with black, brown or white people, or people holding their own religious views. This does not mean the other party is wrong. Try and mix with other people in order to fully understand them and their views.

- Trust and loyalty are the key values. Surround yourself with trusting, loyal people. We are too often blinded by our own expectations of people, situations, or beliefs. Simply be cautious.

- When you start a project, finish it no matter how hard or

difficult. People admire those who have a dream and execute it, but don't be foolish. There may come a time to consider whether to back away, and just accept the loss of money and time should you reach a stage where the risk of success outweighs the loss.

- Ignore those who say you can't do it. Be determined if it's what you really want. Don't give up because the going has got tough. It's maybe like climbing a mountain, and once you get to the top, there is the sweet exhilaration of success and you can see the land in every direction.

- Money comes and goes. It does take time to recover from setbacks, but sometimes this is not the case. But do not look down on someone just because they are not succeeding financially, as that table may well change in an instance when you least expect it. Judge someone on their values, their achievements, and your 'gut' feeling.

- Only once you have perceived honesty should you proceed and consider the financial rewards insofar as any involvement or negotiations. Don't let greed get in the way.

- Revel in your achievements, feel proud of yourself, but don't go off with a superior attitude and shout it to the world. This only brings resentment and situations do sometimes change. Simply enjoy the moment and what you have achieved.

- Treat others with respect, whether they are high or low. What is important is whether their values align with yours and are honest and respectful towards others whatever their circumstances. Not all work is equally remunerated, and money does not equate to friendship and loyalty.

- Remember, success is not determined by the person who is most ruthless or shouts the loudest. Success comes from how you treat others. You may be soft-spoken, but this does not mean you are weak. Often such people are often underestimated, and they may well be the most determined. By so doing you gain respect and admiration.

One of South Africa's richest men once spent an hour with me, chatting and giving advice. People would pay thousands of rands to have a chance to listen to him. He always spoke with a quiet voice and made sense. Then I had a friend who was a pole-holder at my wedding, who made millions, and who was purely focused on money. I asked him to loan me R500 for food for my children when things were really rough, but he said times were tough and he had no money, yet when we bumped into each other he will tell those around that I am his best friend despite the fact that we haven't seen each other for a long while. Who garnered my respect and trust?

- When working try follow your passion, and a 'can do' attitude, but given that the society we live in is a capitalistic one, don't assume that you will be adequately remunerated if you give of your best. You must also fight for the remuneration you think you deserve.

- Look at their character. Blind trust can lead to problems when you are least aware.

- Don't trust simply because you believe the person is more competent and successful than you. If you invest with them keep reviewing the situation. Don't have the attitude that you can now sit back. If anything happens, then it is on your head, and there will be recriminations.

- When you are in a 'black hole' and there seems no light, take time out in nature even if you cannot afford the time to do so. Success comes and goes as do the most unexpected opportunities. Try to move one small step at a time, and not look back and blame yourself. There's that old saying: When you make a decision, it was right at that time, now you must make another decision, and that is right at this time. Don't hanker after what has gone. There are so many new and different things ahead of you.

- Be true to yourself. If you feel you are compromising your values, walk away. Don't just listen and obey like a robot. Your inner heart tells you right from wrong. Listen...

- Aim for the stars. You may not get there but you will have no regrets, and you will at least travel part of the way. Others may try and deter you, but they don't understand your motivation, nor do they have your values, so listen to your inner voice.

- Take out saving or life insurance plans as soon as you can. You never know if you will have children. Further, it may be hard to imagine life in 40 years' time. You probably feel invincible and that you have plenty of time to succeed, but time passes quickly as do opportunities, especially as you age. You will always be grateful for the financial boost in later life through this forced saving mechanism.

- There may be times where you must acquire jobs you feel are beneath you, lesser jobs. Don't look down on them. They will help you get through whatever crisis you are experiencing and help place your feet back on solid ground. You can always upscale later.

- Talk and listen to successful people. Try and surround yourself with such folk, but do not try and compete with them, as this can only bring pain and frustration.

- When someone has failed you, robbed you, tried to harm you in whatever way, the longer you hold a grudge the longer resentment grows and eats away at you. You must move on! Whether you just bury the incident or not, but separate and move on from that person, and in due course don't forget but forgive them. Try and learn from it.

- Set important values for your life and try and live by these values. The Ten Commandments are a great guide.

- Plan before you proceed. Battles are won before the first blow is struck. You have heard the saying, 'The harder I practice, the luckier I become'. So it is in life, plan, plan, plan, and consider all eventualities.

- Don't act out of anger. Someone may cross you, and it may be very hurtful, but before you react, consider whether you can nevertheless benefit from this action. Something is always better than nothing.

- Try not to criticise others even more so if they are older than you. No one likes to be criticised, so try find another way to draw attention to errors whatever they may be.

- 'Read the tea leaves' before you make any decision. The ground is often shifting, so be sure of the outcome when you make your move.

- Some seek riches as a path to fulfilment, others find riches through a life of service. Be awesome in everything you do.

- Should you sell out, take the entire payment at once. Rather lose money than take a time payment. The risk is too great however well you know the buyer as circumstances change.

- Try live your life in balance. That means don't pursue a singular objective. Don't just focus on success, achievements and money. Sacrifice some of this for personal relationships and friendships, for spending time with nature and adventure. You will be surprised how little this will actually affect your ambition and pursuits, whilst it will lead to a more enjoyable life and a more rounded individual.

- Try and stay in the 'now' and take delight in other's successes, however great or small.

In this regard, I have been fortunate to play golf with many prominent stars, and the question arises who did you enjoy most competing with?

There was Bobby Locke, what a thrill. I was also in awe of my hero, Ismail Chowglay, what a role model and so much fun to play with us juniors. Raymond Ackerman was very determined and competitive, despite his age; Rodger Davis so helpful and free with his advice; David Frost against whom I pitted myself and fortunately sunk a long putt from well off the green when being filmed by SuperSport television; Denis Watson knowing he really won the US Open; and my dear friend Sally Little, always encouraging me to start playing seriously again, amongst others, but it may surprise you to know that the three games which standout the most are with three friends:

Big Bernie Schneider, a battler if ever there was one, uncoordinated stiff swing with little pivot, but he had the ability to listen to advice and broke 45 for the first time. We were so excited, then he passed on three days later.

Jonathan 'Japes' Pinshaw with whom I started nursery school and sat every high school break together. Tumours in one leg were such that he had no leg muscle after they were removed. Stiff leg and all he learnt to play and surprised me not only by hitting the ball far but having a brilliant score at Clovelly.

Trevor Zabow who also sat every school break together, and who listened to coaching and broke 90 for the first time to the huge delight of both of us.

I am old but I am forever young at heart. We are always the same age inside. Know that you are the perfect age. Each year is special and precious, you can only live it once. Do not regret growing older, it's a privilege denied to many.
– Richard Gere

DEPRESSION learning how to cope

Do not take depression lightly. It attacks some of the strongest and most successful folk. Why you may ask? Possibly the answer is that we judge ourselves too harshly, we aspire too high, or we believe we have not achieved what we are capable of.

Making mistakes which have cost us dearly is another, be that personal ties, friendship or family, or it relates to a financial situation in which we find ourselves.

It is very difficult to stop once it starts, and the downward spiral seems to accelerate, despite the love and help from those around you.

How do you escape such a medical affliction?

- Go see your medical doctor and received anti-depressant medication. This takes a number of days to kick-in, but it can really make a difference.
- Go see a psychologist. They can help by getting you to let out your emotions, troubles and worries.
- Speak with an understanding friend, if you have one. More than anything, you need to talk and get the 'poison' out.
- Take time out. Sit outside in the sunshine in the garden and listen to the birds. Nature has a wonderful way of healing us. Life simply goes on, and you need to decide whether you wish

to be part of life.

- Whatever you do, you must stop blaming yourself for whatever has befallen you. It is very easy to see mistakes in hindsight, but at the time you made a calculated decision. It was the right decision at that time, but now you must make another decision to go forward, however painful.

- If this involves money, understand that money comes and goes, and can come again. It just takes time. Stop comparing yourself with successful friends. This is your life, not theirs! Focus on your own accomplishments from bringing up children, to business, sport, and romantic successes.

- No one can get you out of a depression. You must do this yourself by taking one tiny step at a time. I know you will want to stay in bed and hide under the covers, being thankful when the evening darkness arrives, and you can relax and go to sleep. However, you must get up, have a shower, get dressed, brush your teeth and your hair. These are all tiny steps. As you make progress your confidence returns, and you start feeling stronger.

- Taking part whether you succeed or not is a win, so be proud of what you have achieved. Some folk will simply bury the coin in the ground and never accomplish anything.

- If all things fail take out a paint brush, some paint, and a canvass and give it a good. It will distract you, and let time pass.

ADDENDUM: Examples of Messages of Support
SOUTHERN AFRICA GOLF MUSEUM

"There are displays of memorabilia at the South African Museum of Golf that can only be bettered at the R&A museum at St. Andrews and at Royal Blackheath. It should be compulsory for all young golfers to pay the museum a visit so that they can stroll through the history of the game in South Africa". When you came to me and proposed launching the Golf Hall of Fame I gave you absolutely no chance of succeeding. Well you have proved me wrong. This is truly an amazing event and what you have achieved is beyond our wildest dream. Fantastic! Well done Barry. **Dale Hayes**

"I am proud and honoured to be a member of the Southern Africa Golf Hall of Fame which is a tribute to and a record of the achievements and contributions made to our great game. The spectacular Hall of Fame Museum at Oubaai is a must to see - be you a golfer or not." **Hugh Baiocchi**

The completion of the Southern African Golf Hall of Fame Museum brings the history of Southern African Golf up to the level of leading golfing nations, and ahead of many others. Golf history is a major asset to future generations to see how the game of golf has evolved and is an inspiration to new potential champions and all golf fans. Brilliant effort! **Cobie Legrange**

"The Southern Africa Golf Hall of Fame & Museum does a wonderful job at preserving and showcasing our rich golfing heritage. I'm honoured to be alongside so many greats of the game and hope that this can inspire & motivate young Southern African golfers to carry on our great golfing tradition" **Retief Goosen.**

"The Southern African Hall of fame Museum has certainly given the Golf enthusiast in South Africa a wonderful place to visit and see heritage in its finest form. From early beginnings of our Golf course construction to eras of great players years, you will certainly enjoy a collection of memorabilia second to none. If you haven't been its time to visit Oubaai & The Hall of Fame." **Mark McNulty**

"To me, the most important thing in golf is the history and integrity of the game. The Southern African Golf Hall of Fame provides all golf enthusiasts with the opportunity to understand the rich history that we have here. Before the creation of the Hall of Fame, we didn't realize how much valuable history we had sitting right here on our shores. I'm proud to be a part of it." **Sally Little**

Thanks to the vision of Harry Brews and Barry Cohen, South African golf has a Hall of Fame of its own. Players, fans and future generations will be able to enjoy our history and the ongoing story of this wonderful game. **Denis Hutchinson**

'It is one of the proudest moments of my golfing career to be inducted into the Southern African Golf Hall of Fame. I'd like to thank the trustees of the South African Golf Heritage Trust and especially Barry Cohen for all their hard work and effort in preserving the history and continuing the legacy of golf in South Africa for future generations! **John Bland**

"It was a huge honour being inducted into the Southern Africa Hall of Fame in 2009 at their gala dinner. The wonderful artifacts at the Museum allows people to see the wonderful history of the game and learn more about the inductees all in a great setting. Well done my man! **Ernie Els**

I just wanted to let you know how much I appreciate the excellent job you did and the hospitality I received at the South African Golf Heritage Trust's "official opening" of the South African Museum of Golf. I am happy to know that your legacy is spreading. Your expertise and hard work made the event a success, as evidenced by the attendance.

There is only one thing left to say and that is BLOODY AWESOME. I was totally Blown Away last night. Barry you are an Amazing person and to have pulled this off last night was Fantastic (Golf Hall of Fame) when many thought you were Crazy. But you did it. Great job, well done! CONGRATULATIONS **Alan Shuman** (Director Brandhouse: Bells)

To my Dearest Friend Barry Boy, I am just phoning you to thank you for a fabulous evening. We had so much fun, and it was an amazing evening. I am so proud of you! All my love, **Sally Little**

Wendy and I just would like to congratulate you on the "Hall of Fame" Induction affair on Friday – it really was a great evening! **Raymond Ackerman**

BOOK REVIEWS

Blazing the Trail

I implore all South Africans to read this book! Against all odds, the story of black golf in South Africa must be told. Definitely the President would love that he is a golfer. **SA Minister of Sport Tokozile Xasa**

Thank you for this wonderful addition to my library Barry. it is sincerely appreciated. I enjoyed expanding my knowledge and understanding of this chapter in our South African Golfing History. It was certainly a labour of love for you Barry. In your note you say that this is your Final Chapter Barry... I suggest not. I have always been of the opinion, and continue to champion that the Papwa Sewgolum and Graham Wulff friendship and adventurous success story needs to scripted for the big screen. Flying across the vast African Continent in a single prop Piper Comanche, without GPS and mobile connectivity luxuries... and then winning the Dutch Open makes for an epic sporting movie. **Johan Immelman** (Former Commissioner Sunshine Tour, Trevor's father)

Job well done Barry John Cohen with this publication....I hope the SA Golf Hall of Fame find strong feet for many more years to come in exposing the apartheid government's atrocities against black world class golfers that were never given their dues.... **Mabandla Kelengeshe** (PA Minister of Sport)

Congratulations on a magnificent achievement. It is a story that needed telling. I can vouch for the fact that the book is an excellent read. Outstanding Bazza. Well deserved praise. A must read. **Jonathan Pinshaw** (Australian business guru)

There is arguably no-one better than Barry Cohen to tell this extraordinary tale. This book is not about golf. It uses the history of golf in South Africa to tell remarkable stories of injustice, triumph and camaraderie. And ultimately of the fact that people who seek out commonalities as opposed to differences win at the game of 'life'. **Marc Dhalluin** (former CEO Highbury media)

In a clear and often poetic description of golf, both at the grass roots and at the highest international level, Barry Cohen's book fills an historical void. His book expounds a story that has deserved to be told for many years, not only to demonstrate the extraordinary bravery and resilience of an oppressed majority, but also to highlight the truly exceptional golfers that came from South Africa's caddy ranks. It is perhaps a measure of the restrictive success of the apartheid regime that the names of some of South Africa's finest golfers are virtually unknown outside the country and beat many of the best South African golfers of his time, among them Gary Player.

This history is unusual in that it unavoidably demonstrates the playing of golf as a political activity. It is a measure of South Africa's non-European golfers that they did not allow their political restriction to affect their determination to play the game they loved.

There are many other golfers who resisted the attempts of the Verwoerd and Vorster régime to marginalise or curtail their achievements. All of them are powerfully and clearly described in Mr. Cohen's book.

It is perhaps in the recording of such achievements and playing records that this description will in the future be most valuable. Although much of the history that Mr. Cohen describes is relatively recent, much of it was suppressed or not recorded at the time. Future historians will thank him for the scrupulous way in which he has recorded the playing prowess and successes of non-European golfers, although the inclusion of an index would improve any further editions. Without these records, to some extent at least the apartheid philosophy would have succeeded in air-brushing out the achievements of non-white golfers. Future historians have in Barry Cohen's book a considerable resource on which to draw. Behind each achievement their lies a story that enriches golf history.

Barry Cohen's book opens our eyes to the many strictures and slights imposed on non-Europeans within the world of golf, but it also brings to our notice the exceptional courage of those who rose above such policies and with tenacity and dignity demonstrated that golf could be played by all parts of society, and that given the chance South Africa had talented golfers of all races who could compete with the best in the world.

This is a book that is clear and easily read. In many instances its content is disturbing, but it shows a parallel history to the previously received history of South African golf, which should be understood more widely by golf historians. I hope that it will be widely read by all those with an interest in the game's history. It deserves no less. **Roger McStravich** (two-time winner Herbert Warren Wind book award from the United States Golf Association)

Cohen's intricately researched book offers rare insight into the history of black golf from even before apartheid, long before the more recent stars like Papwa Sewgolum and Vincent Tshabalala. It's a collection of gems of information. **Sunday Times** (David Isaacson)

A new book celebrates the forgotten stars of SA golf – maligned and discriminated against for their colour Cohen brings deep sensitivity to the stories of golf's dispossessed caddies who were often self-taught on improvised "clubs". Cohen tells them all with great energy and dedication; they make for a fascinating read. It's a collection of gems of information. **Business Day** (Luke Alfred)

Barry, Your excellent book. Congratulations, I have very much enjoyed reading your book and learning so much from its content. I am sure that there is more information that you will continue to gather. Future historians will undoubtedly thank you for doing so. **Through the Green UK** (Mungo Park)

Blazing the Trail is the story interwoven with the history and statistics of 90 years of black golf largely undocumented and untold until now. This is not only the blow-by-blow account of tournaments, but also the narrative of how players rose above the challenges only for those in authority to stop the sweeping winds of change. Compleat Golfer (Craig Ray)

The stories are compelling, the history fascinating, and kudos to Barry Cohen for bringing both to light. Blazing the Trail is a wonderful tribute to those forgotten champions and an inspiration to us all. Great read. I really learnt so much. Highly recommended. **Sally Little** (2-time LPGA Major winner, 15 LPGA titles)

I absolutely loved this book. Barry Cohen did amazing research on all of the great golfers who had the misfortune of being affected by the Apartheid policy. There is Papwa Sewgolum winning three Dutch Opens, two Natal Opens, and coming very close to conquering the SA Open. Then there is my favourite, Vincent Tshabalala's French Open, which I believe is the gutsiest performance of all time. He could not afford a caddy so lugged his own clubs, yet still won on Le Touquet La Mer, no small feat. Other heroes like Ismail Chowglay, Simon Hlapo, and more. If you want to learn about the forgotten heroes of golf and wonder what might have been had their circumstances been different, or are just a lover of golf or sports history in general, this is a must read. **Amazon 5* Tad Deja**

A GREAT and easy read even for non golfer to enjoy about another tragedy that Apartheid imposed......Well done and exceptionally researched. This is really well worth the read. But where Barry researched and got the info from just blows me away... **Bernard Schneider**

Great read. This book is easily understood by those who don't know much about golf, yet the message is of hope and perseverance.

It tells the story so that these golfers and their struggles are not forgotten, and in so doing, it creates black golfing heroes to inspire the youth, whilst recording the lost history of those who were disadvantaged during the Apartheid years. Well done on such a fine book. An excellent read. **Rajen Sewgolum** ('Papwa' Sewgolum's son)

INDEX

Made in the USA
Monee, IL
07 July 2026

56552242R00152